LIVING FROM
FAITH TO FAITH

LIVING FROM FAITH TO FAITH

A Compilation of Sermons for Spiritual Growth and Inspiration

Dr. Gloria Ann Turner

authorHOUSE®

AuthorHouse™
1663 Liberty Drive
Bloomington, IN 47403
www.authorhouse.com
Phone: 1-800-839-8640

© 2012 by Dr. Gloria Ann Turner. All rights reserved.

No part of this book may be reproduced, stored in a retrieval system, or transmitted by any means without the written permission of the author.

Published by AuthorHouse   05/02/2012

ISBN: 978-1-4685-6436-5 (sc)
ISBN: 978-1-4685-6435-8 (hc)
ISBN: 978-1-4685-6434-1 (e)

Library of Congress Control Number: 2012904691

Any people depicted in stock imagery provided by Thinkstock are models, and such images are being used for illustrative purposes only.
Certain stock imagery © Thinkstock.

This book is printed on acid-free paper.

Because of the dynamic nature of the Internet, any web addresses or links contained in this book may have changed since publication and may no longer be valid. The views expressed in this work are solely those of the author and do not necessarily reflect the views of the publisher, and the publisher hereby disclaims any responsibility for them.

Scripture quotations are from the Holy Bible, New International Version®, (NIV), copyright © 1973, 1978, and 1984 by the International Bible Society. Used by permission of Zondervan. All rights reserved.

Scripture quotations are from the Holy Bible, New King James Version, (NKJV), copyright © 1979, 1980, and 1982 by Thomas Nelson, Inc. Used by permission. All rights reserved.

Scripture quotations are from the Holy Bible, King James Version, (KJV).

Front and back cover designed by Nailah Turner

DEDICATION

This book is dedicated to my husband Robert, daughter TiNese, son Michael, daughter-in-law Nailah, and grandson Brandon, who are my inspiration in everything I do and every choice I make. I also dedicate this book to my mom Laura and dad Dewayne, who always supported me in every endeavor. I thank God for everyone who has given me the opportunity to be a channel for change in their personal spiritual growth and those who have touched me in a special way. Much Love!

Contents

Acknowledgments ix

Introduction xi

Sermon One   Follow The Yellow Brick Road 1

Sermon Two   Chosen By God... 11

Sermon Three   Fight Fear With Faith............................... 21

Sermon Four   I Know A Place.. 29

Sermon Five   A Changed Life... 37

Sermon Six   True Worshipers....................................... 45

Sermon Seven   Stay Focused 53

Sermon Eight   Does God Show Favoritism? 61

Sermon Nine   Exercise Your Faith 69

Sermon Ten   The Glory Of Seeking Jesus................. 77

Sermon Eleven   You Can Have What You Want 83

Sermon Twelve   The Unknown Son 93

Conclusion 103

About The Author 105

ACKNOWLEDGMENTS

First, I would like to thank God, my Heavenly Father, who laid this on my heart. From the beginning to the end, the Lord in His wisdom guided me in writing each line. The Lord has taught me by the power of His Spirit how to preach and teach the gospel of Jesus Christ.

Secondly, I thank God for the people that He has placed in my life over the years. Each one of the friends and special colleagues that I have met during my years as a public relations specialist, as a college professor, as a minister of the gospel, and as an author has contributed in nurturing me for the greater works of God.

Finally, I pray that everyone who reads these sermons will be inspired to give more of themselves to God and less to the world.

INTRODUCTION

After earning a doctorate in theology at Chesapeake Bible College and Seminary of Ridgely, Maryland, I had a strong desire to publish a book. I thought about writing a spiritual devotion guide from my dissertation on the topic, "Who Touched Me?: Understanding the Manifestation of the Spiritual Gifts of the Holy Spirit." However, in June 2011 while writing a sermon for the following Sunday, I realized that I had sermons on multiple computers. With the help of my grandson Brandon, I collected them from the various computers and placed them in one file on my laptop. In the midst of this compilation process, I discovered that I was preparing to preach my one-hundredth sermon. I thought to myself, *what a wonderful milestone*.

During that week, the Holy Spirit spoke to me about publishing twelve of my sermons under the title <u>Living From Faith to Faith</u>. I was overwhelmed with joy! This collection of twelve sermons speaks eloquently to the scripture: "For therein is the righteousness of God revealed from faith to faith: as it is written, THE JUST SHALL LIVE BY FAITH" (Romans 1:17). Each sermon is prepared to help you, dear reader, apply a practical and workable operation of faith in your life—a faith that works. Understanding true biblical faith is the key to receiving God's

Dr. Gloria Ann Turner

promises. You will witness the presence and power of the Holy Spirit within each page of this book.

I pray that each sermon will speak to your spirit and bring forth God's anointing to help you build a stronger foundation of faith in your life. Also, I pray that each sermon will bring you to a closer encounter with God that leaves you with a deeper commitment to do God's work.

These sermons were preached at various locations, with many people requesting CDs or DVDs of them. I am so happy to make them available to you in this book.

Sermon One

FOLLOW THE YELLOW BRICK ROAD

"Life's Journey"
Scripture Reading: Matthew 7:13-14

Enter through the narrow gate. For wide is the gate and broad is the road that leads to destruction, and many enter through it. But small is the gate and narrow the road that leads to life, and only a few find it.

One of the greatest American films in history is <u>The Wizard of Oz</u>. As you may recall, the main character is a lonely and sad Kansas farm girl named Dorothy. In the beginning, Dorothy talks about going to a place where there isn't any trouble. She asks her pet dog, "Do you suppose there is such a place, Toto?" She concludes that there must be a place, "over the rainbow," where there are no problems. During a terrible tornado, Dorothy is struck on the head and transported to a land beyond the rainbow.

Dr. Gloria Ann Turner

In this new world called the Land of Oz, she meets several magical characters who give her specific instructions to follow the yellow brick road. This path will lead her to the Emerald City, where the Wizard can assist her in getting home. While traveling down the yellow brick road, she meets the Scarecrow, the Tin Man, and the Cowardly Lion. During their trip to the Emerald City, she defeats the Wicked Witch of the West. When they arrive at the gates of the Emerald City, they are told that no one can see the great Oz, and that nobody has ever seen the great Oz. By the end of the movie, however, Dorothy and her friends gain access to the Wizard, and he gives them their hearts' desires: the Scarecrow gets a brain, the Tin Man gets a heart, the Lion gets courage, and Dorothy gets to return home to Kansas.

If we look into the scriptures, everyone is on a journey as he or she travels through life, and not just any journey. Everyone is on a spiritual journey that will lead them to an eternal home. Every day, we make choices that will affect the direction we are headed on our spiritual journey. Several people think the roads we can choose to travel are many. That may seem true, but from a biblical perspective, there are really only two roads to travel and you must choose between them.

In Jesus' sermon on Mount Zion, He spoke of two roads. Each road has its own beginning and ending. One road is heavily populated; the other road traveled only by a few. Let's look closely at the text and see how Jesus describes the differences between two gates, two roads, and ultimately, two destinations.

The Two Gates

Jesus opens with the statement, "Enter through the narrow gate." However, He begins the discussion with the wide gate instead of the narrow gate. Jesus continues, "For wide is the gate . . . that leads to destruction and many enter through it." This wide gate represents the spiritual journey that leads to eternal death. Evidently, it is described as "wide" because this gate allows many people to enter with no sacrifice on their part. Those entering through the wide gate are not required to give up anything; everything can fit through the wide gate. One is allowed to bring along whatever "baggage" he or she has. This baggage is filled with the lust and wickedness of the world. The spirits of pride, hatred, jealousy, envy, unforgiveness, greediness, and lust are rampant. Every day, television, movies, billboards, newspapers, and magazines bombard us with lustful images. When lustful thoughts become part of our lifestyle, we feel like prisoners to those controlling desires. God does not want us to be a prisoner of lust and evil. The Bible tells us that "Christ has made us free" (Galatians 5:1). We have assurance from our Lord that He will help us battle lust and the evil things of this world.

The wide gate allows people to believe whatever they want to believe. Most people choose to travel through the wide gate because there are no restrictions concerning belief and behavior. Some believe in witchcraft, palm reading, rabbits' feet, or the Da Vinci Code. It is a wide gate because anything and everything can come through it. Please understand that the more you indulge in sin, the easier it is to access the wide gate. Make no mistake, the wide gate is owned by Satan.

Jesus said, "But small is the gate . . . that leads to life and only a few find it." The small gate represents the spiritual journey that leads to eternal life. Why is it small? It is a small gate because it requires us to be obedient to God and to practice self-denial. "If you love me, keep my commandments" (John 14:15). In Matthew 16:24, Jesus said, "If anyone would come after me, he must deny himself and take up his cross and follow me." Also, the Lord spoke these words in John 10:9, "I am the gate; whoever enters through me will be saved. He will come in and go out, and find pasture." Many people have accepted Jesus as their Savior, but they have failed to establish a relationship with Him that will give them divine directions on how to travel the Christian journey. They continue to lust after earthly goods instead of pursuing the things of God. In Matthew 6:19-21, the scripture clearly says, "Do not store up for yourselves treasures on earth, where moth and rust destroy, and where thieves break in and steal. But store up for yourselves treasures in heaven, where moth and rust do not destroy, and where thieves do not break in and steal. For where your treasure is, there your heart will be also."

The small gate has no room for an unforgiving spirit. The Lord taught an important lesson in Matthew 6:14-15, "For if you forgive men when they sin against you, your heavenly Father will also forgive you. But if you do not forgive men their sins, your Father will not forgive your sins." One must demonstrate a loving, compassionate, and forgiving spirit. The small gate has no room for self-righteousness. In Matthew 6:1,

Jesus instructs His disciples to "be careful not to do your acts of righteousness before men, to be seen by them. If you do, you will have no reward from your Father in heaven." The small gate is the Lord's gate.

I've discussed the wide and small gates. Let's examine the second point Jesus makes about the broad and narrow roads.

The Two Roads

Jesus says, ". . . broad is the road that leads to destruction." The broad road allows any performance one desires. There is no need for spiritual reformation or transformation; people do not need to change their sinful lifestyles. The world has a welcome sign for the unbelievers. It says, "Come as you are! No changes necessary! This way is easy!" On this road, people can make up their own rules and regulations. They can promote their selfish ways and thoughts. Many people love this broad road. The people of Sodom and Gomorrah traveled this road, and they were all destroyed. This road gives a false impression that people are "open-minded" and "free" to experience better times. They label themselves as "tolerant" of others. This broad road has unnecessary pain and problems. There is nothing on this road that God has for you. This path is for those who love the things of the world, and it leads to eternal damnation. The Word says, "Do not love the world or anything in the world. If anyone loves the world, the love of the Father is not in him. For everything in the world—the cravings of sinful man, the lust of his eyes, and the boasting of what he has and does—comes not from the Father but from the world. The world and its desires will pass away, but the man who does the will of God lives forever" (1 John 2:15-17). However, the good news is that Jesus came so you do not have to travel this road. In John 14:6, Jesus exerts, "I am the way, the truth and the life. No one comes to the Father except through me." Also in John 10:10, Jesus states, "I have come that they may have life and have it to the full."

    The small gate directs people to the narrow road that leads to life. The narrow road is not an easy way. It is a path that leads to life, and it is difficult because it requires putting God first and not yourself. For instance, one must accept Jesus Christ as Lord and Savior. However, one not only accepts Jesus, but one begins a lifelong relationship with Him. The path requires holy and righteous living, which means to pick up his or her cross and follow Jesus. It requires knowing the voice of Jesus and being obedient to Him. Jesus illustrates this point in John 10:14-17, when he declares that "He knows his sheep and his sheep know Him." Jesus continues, "My sheep listen to my voice; I know them, and they follow me" (John 10:27). They will not follow anyone else. As a follower of Christ, we have responsibilities on this narrow road. We must witness to the unsaved about Jesus' life, death, burial, and resurrection. We must develop a praying spirit, advance in our knowledge of the scriptures, and fellowship with other believers as often as possible. It is a road that requires change. We must change our natural selfishness to unselfishness, change our negative attitudes to positive, and change our abhorrence to love. We need to show the world that we are in this world, but we are not of this world.

As Christians, we are called to love all people, regardless of faith, lifestyle or gender orientation in the same way that God loves all people. He provides guidelines for living as found in the Holy Scriptures and we support those guidelines as a people called to love and obey His calling upon our lives. Jesus invites all people to change their lives and come into His dimension, but not all will come. We are called to model what Christ taught when He prayed that what was in heaven would be manifested on earth through a people known for their love of one another and others. A song writer wrote, "A wonderful change has come over me." Because of its godly requirements, many people choose not to travel this road. They think it's too hard; it's too "confining." But, Jesus tells us to strive to enter through the small gate and travel the narrow road. This is the same road that Jesus traveled and paved the way for us. Jesus gave his life for us on this narrow road. This is a purpose-driven road of joy, happiness, peace, and prosperity. Jesus said, "I came that you may have life and have it more abundantly" (John 10:10).

The final point that Jesus makes in this passage of scripture is the existence of two destinations: eternal destruction and eternal life.

Two Destinations

Jesus said, "Wide is the gate, broad is the road that leads to destruction, and many go in by it." This destination is one of total devastation, eternal hell. Eternity in hell is reserved for those who reject Jesus Christ and His Gospel. The Bible sums up the Gospel in 1 Corinthians 15:3-4, "For what I received I passed on to you as of first importance that Christ died for our sins according to the Scriptures, that he was buried, that he was raised on the third day according to the Scriptures." We have all sinned and cannot live up to God's holiness. Romans 3:23 says, "For all have sinned and fall short of the glory of God." The destination to hell is described in the Bible as a lake of fire burning endlessly. Romans 6:23 tells us the penalty for our sin, "For the wages of sin is death, but the gift of God is eternal life in Christ Jesus our Lord." There is only pain and never relief. Paul wrote in 2 Thessalonians 1:7-9 about the everlasting destruction that is to come. It will come upon those who do not know God—those who have not accepted the Lord Jesus Christ. It will come upon those who do not obey the gospel of Jesus Christ. John described it as "a lake of fire." This destination is eternal hell. When one enters, one cannot exit.

Thanks be to God that the Scriptures urge us to enter the narrow road that leads to life. God sent His Son, Jesus Christ, to die in our place so we could be spared from Hell. Romans 5:8 says, "But God demonstrates his own love for us in this: While we were still sinners, Christ died for us." According to the Bible, we aren't required to subscribe to a religious formula or do more good things than bad ones. God gives His gift freely to all who ask. "Everyone who calls on the name of the Lord will be saved" (Romans 10:13). This alternate destination is life; it is the "gift of God." God wants everyone on this road that leads to eternal heaven. 1 John 5:11-13 says, "And this is the testimony: God has given us eternal life, and this life is in his

Son. He who has the Son has life; he who does not have the Son of God does not have life. I write these things to you who believe in the name of the Son of God so that you may know that you have eternal life." Do you know for sure that you will spend eternal life with God in heaven? If not, this is a decision you don't want to put off.

Dorothy knew where she wanted to go and how she needed to get there. She had to follow the yellow brick road. God has laid out a perfect plan for us to follow. He wants us to come to Jesus, receive eternal life, and live an abundant life on earth. We, too, must follow God's yellow brick road which we enter through the small gate that leads to God's narrow path. If people would travel the narrow road, they would experience the blessed life that's promised to us through the covenant of God. PRAISE THE LORD! AMEN.

LET'S PRAY TOGETHER

Heavenly Father,

We thank You for Christ's victory on the Cross that opened the way for us to have a loving and fulfilling relationship with You. Help us to travel our divine journey by faith with the power of the Holy Spirit. We ask You to count us worthy of our calling and to enable us to fulfill Your purposes, through the grace, faith, and authority we have in Christ. In Jesus' name, Amen.

Sermon Two

CHOSEN BY GOD

"Leadership"
Scripture Reading: Numbers 27:15-20

Moses said to the Lord, "May the Lord, the God of the spirits of all mankind, appoint a man over this community to go out and come in before them, one who will lead them out and bring them in, so the Lord's people will not be like sheep without a shepherd." So the Lord said to Moses, "Take Joshua, son of Nun, a man in whom is the spirit, and lay your hand on him. Have him stand before Eleazar, the priest, and the entire assembly and commission him in their presence. Give him some of your authority so the whole Israelite community will obey him."

In our knowledge-driven world, the power to lead is shifting to the power to promote new ideas and better ways based on innovation. Now, the meaning of leadership is simply the successful promotion of new directions. Leaders show the way. This definition of leadership is consistent with market leadership or leadership in sports where one individual, team, or organization "shows the way" for others. Leadership fascinates people. New leadership brings new people, fresh ideas, and different styles which come to the forefront of the product. New leadership brings hope for some and frustration and disappointment for others. Everywhere, people are hungry for power, position, and possession. People will pursue positions of power and authority because they want to be in charge. The power to lead runs deep, and in the wrong hands, it can be dangerous. However, that is not Jesus' idea of leadership. Jesus is not primarily interested in what a spiritual leader accomplishes. He is more interested in the character of the man or woman. Why? The reason is that leaders should set an example of acceptable conduct for others to follow. Leaders stand in the place of Jesus as spiritual shepherds. Jesus is more interested in a man's heart than in all of his activities (1 Sam. 15:22; Hosea 6:6; Matt. 9:13; Matt. 15:17-20). Jesus called the disciples together and said, "You know that the rulers of the Gentiles lord it over them, and their high officials exercise authority over them. Not so with you. Instead, whoever wants to become great among you must be your servant, and whoever wants to be first must be your slave—just as the Son of Man did not come to be served, but to serve, and to give his life as a ransom for many" (Matthew 20:25-28).

    The Book of Numbers is the fourth book of the Pentateuch. Moses wrote Numbers shortly before his death in 1406 B.C. The name, Numbers, comes from two censuses taken of the

Israelites during their thirty-eight years of wandering the wilderness, found in chapters one and twenty-six. The book is divided into three parts, each being related to one of the major campsites of the Israelites: nineteen days in the Sinai wilderness (Numbers 1:1-10:10); thirty-eight years between the wilderness and the plains of Moab (10:11—21:35); and roughly five months on the plains of Moab (22:1-36:13). Numbers relates the story of the Israelites' journey from Mount Sinai to the plains of Moab on the border of Canaan. Numbers tells of the complaining, murmuring, rebellion, disobedience, and judgment of the Israelites. Because of their constant disobedience, they were condemned to live out their lives in the desert. Only their children would enjoy the fulfillment of the promise that had originally been theirs. Throughout the years in the desert, one thing became clear to the Israelites: God's constant care for them. No matter what they did wrong, God provided for them. Not only did He meet their needs, but He also loved and forgave His people continually. That's an incredible kind of love. Who wouldn't want to serve a God like that?

In the Hebrew Scriptures, we meet two important leaders. The first leader is Moses. The Lord commanded Moses to go up to Mt. Nebo and see the land that he would give the Israelites. Moses surveyed the land and saw that it was good. What an extraordinary irony that after all Moses had been through, after all of the insults and persecution he endured, after all of the miracles he performed through the power of God, after all that he had done, this was as far as he was allowed to go. God told Moses to look at the Promised Land, but not to enter it. The reason behind this is found in Numbers 20:8 when the Lord told Moses, "Take the staff, and you and your brother Aaron gather the assembly together. Speak to that rock before their eyes and it will pour out its water. You will bring water out of the rock for the community so they and their livestock can drink." Numbers 20:9-11 records Moses' response, "So Moses took the staff from the Lord's presence, just as He commanded him. He and Aaron gathered the assembly together in front of the rock and Moses said to them, 'Listen, you rebels, must we bring you water out of this rock?' Then Moses raised his arm and struck the rock twice with his staff. Water gushed out, and the community and their livestock drank." Numbers 20:12 gives us the Lord's response to Moses' actions, "Because you did not trust in me enough to honor me as holy in the sight of the Israelites, you will not bring this community into the land I give them."

Please do not conclude, even for a moment, that Moses was a failure. No, Moses was a giant of a man. He had an extraordinary ministry. Everything that the Bible tells us about him makes that clear. His stature among the people, his concern for the people, his personal integrity, and his dedication to God kept him from being just an ordinary individual. He demonstrated great leadership. As we saw by Moses' response to the oppression of his fellow Jews, he certainly did possess leadership qualities. Moses was the most humble of men and became the finest leader and the greatest teacher of the Israelites. Furthermore, despite his upbringing, Moses rejected his role in Egyptian society, as well as the culture and beliefs of Egypt. This is evidenced by the fact that after leaving Egypt, we are told, "And Moses was the shepherd of his father-in-law's flock" (Exodus 3:1). Notice his epitaph (the inscription on his tombstone) at the very end of the Pentateuch: "Since then, no prophet has risen in Israel like Moses, whom the Lord knew face to face, who did all those miraculous signs and wonders the Lord sent him to do in Egypt—to Pharaoh and to all his officials and to his whole land. For no one has ever shown the mighty power or performed the awesome deeds that Moses did in the sight of all Israel" (Deuteronomy 34:10-12). Moses was chosen by God, and God made known His ways and deeds to him.

For a few minutes, I want you to think about what will be written about you in your obituary or on your tombstone. Will it have only your name, date of birth, and date of departure? I don't know about you, but I want the words "Gloria Ann Turner lived a life of faith, and she walked with God," to be written on mine. The Bible tells us that Enoch and Noah walked with God. Everyone should have the desire to walk with God. More than that, God wants us to walk with Him.

Moses did not live forever, but in his death, there is a lesson. The lesson is this: God is in charge of life and death. He is Alpha and Omega, the Beginning and the End, the First and the Last. God is committed only to God's way. God is not committed to any person. God is not committed to any individual's program. God is not committed to our degrees. God is not committed to our money or any political power we may have, or think we have. No, what concerns God are His purpose and plan. God blesses His work, done in His power through Jesus.

Dr. Gloria Ann Turner

For just a moment, let us examine the Book of Numbers, chapter twenty-seven, verses sixteen and seventeen. After God told Moses that he was not to cross into the Promised Land, Moses was very humble and expressed concern for the people of Israel. He offered this prayer for his people: "May the Lord, the God of the spirits of all mankind, appoint a man over this community to go out and come in before them, one who will lead them out and bring them in, so that the Lord's people will not be like sheep without a shepherd." God answered Moses' prayer. He appointed Joshua to be Moses' successor. "Now after the death of Moses the servant of the Lord it came to pass, that the Lord spake unto Joshua the son of Nun, Moses' minister, saying, 'Moses my servant is dead; now therefore arise, go over this Jordan, thou, and all this people, unto the land which I do give to them, even to the children of Israel'" (Joshua 1:1-2). Joshua was the new leader. It is important that we constantly pray for our church leaders and national leaders because God is a God who answers prayer. Jesus told us in Matthew 21:22, "If you believe, you will receive whatever you ask for in prayer." We must pray and believe in God.

Joshua was no stranger to Moses; they had forty years of service and fellowship together. God spent many years preparing Joshua for this new responsibility of leadership. Joshua was born a slave in Egypt. His parents named him Hoshea, which means "Salvation." That was really an act of faith on their part, because they were in bondage; they had no control over their lives or their future, yet they claimed the promise that God had made to Abraham many years before that there would be salvation from Egypt. Years later, Moses changed Hoshea's name to Joshua, which means "Yahweh is Salvation." Joshua is the Hebrew form of the name Jesus. Joshua was the oldest son of a man named Nun of the tribe of Ephraim. The fact that Joshua was the firstborn meant his life would have been in danger on the night of Passover, but Joshua and his family had faith in the Lord and brushed the blood of a lamb over the doorpost to be protected. As a young man, Joshua saw all the signs and wonders that God performed in Egypt. He had an increasing awareness in that Yahweh was a God of power who would care for His people. He saw God humiliate the demonic gods of Egypt, demonstrating that He alone was the true God. Joshua saw God roll back the waters of the Red Sea to save Israel, and then close those same waters to drown Pharaoh's army. Through all of that, Joshua became a man of faith, knowing the Lord and trusting Him as the God of deliverance.

Joshua was probably in his eighties at that time. Throughout Exodus and Numbers, we see him in many roles. We have seen him as a soldier, a spy, a servant, and a minister to Moses. He was ultimately chosen by God to take His people into the Promised Land. The same anointing that was on Moses fell upon Joshua. It was the anointing of Jesus Christ because He was with God in the beginning when He created the heaven and the earth. When God assigns someone to a certain task, He will equip that person with an anointing to carry out that task. This reminds me of another principle of God. God chooses whom He wants to be the leader. It is not for us to decide who will lead the people. While people are busy looking at the outer appearance of people, God is looking at the heart. Do you remember what the Lord told Samuel as he was looking at the sons of Jesse to anoint as the next king of Israel? He told Samuel: "Do not consider his appearance or his height, for I have rejected him. The Lord does not look at the things people look at. People look at the outward appearance, but the Lord looks at the heart" (1 Samuel 16:7). He chooses the right person, at the right time, to do the right thing. If God is for you, who can be against you? Just like God prepared Joshua, God will prepare you to take your position in the church and the community. God will equip, train, and teach you everything you need to lead. God told his prophet Jeremiah, "Before I formed you in the womb I knew you, before you were born I set you apart, I appointed you as a prophet to the nations" (Jeremiah 1:4-5). Remember, what God has for you is *for you*!

To become an effective leader, you must have a relationship with the Lord. The relationship gives you spiritual authority. God told Moses to give Joshua some of his authority so that the Israelite community would obey him. God's leaders have authority, but it is an authority that stems from God, not from man. God's leaders are called to function in the context of the supernatural, doing things that man alone cannot do.

When Joshua became the leader after Moses' death, God spoke these wonderful reassuring words to him: "No one will be able to stand up against you all the days of your life. As I was with Moses, so I will be with you; I will never leave you or forsake you" (Joshua 1:5). These same words apply to us today when God appoints us to a task. God will give us the strength to stand up against anything. God will be with us, and He will never leave us or forsake us.

New leadership of any kind is hard, but God is the author of leadership. The power to lead comes from within, where the Holy Spirit resides. As a leader, one should expect oppositions, problems, and challenges. Conflicts help bring forth resolutions. If God has chosen you to lead, remember these words: "You, dear children, are from God and have overcome them (opposition), because the one who is in you is greater than the one who is in the world" (1 John 4:4). PRAISE THE LORD! AMEN.

LET'S PRAY TOGETHER

Gracious Father,

We acknowledge that You are a holy and righteous God. We thank You for Your precious anointing that gives us the power to accomplish our divine mission. We realize that we cannot lead others without the power of the Holy Spirit directing and guiding us. Thank You for the privilege of being able to enter with confidence into the place where You dwell, because of the atonement that Jesus has made on our behalf. In Jesus' name, Amen.

Sermon Three

FIGHT FEAR WITH FAITH

"Faith at Work"
Scripture Reading: Exodus 1:15-20

The king of Egypt said to the Hebrew midwives, whose names were Shiphrah and Puah, "When you help the Hebrew women in childbirth and observe them on the delivery stool, if it is a boy kill him; but if it is a girl, let her live." The midwives, however, feared God and did not do what the king of Egypt had told them to do; they let the boys live. Then the king of Egypt summoned the midwives and asked them, "Why have you done this? Why have you let the boys live?" The midwives answered Pharaoh, "Hebrew women are not like Egyptian women; they are vigorous and give birth before the midwives arrive." So God was kind to the midwives and the people increased and became even more numerous.

Most of us know what fear is and the harm it can cause. Fear is more than a mental state. It affects both the physiology of the body and the chemical balance within the brain. It is important for you to understand that fear is a spirit, and it is not sent by God. When people are afraid, it generates stress. Extreme stress can manifest itself physically in a number of ways. In extreme cases, it can cause tunnel vision or loss of color perception (color blindness); it can also cause a distortion of both time and depth perception. When people are involved in a serious car accident, they tend to describe these effects. They may say, "It was like everything was in slow motion," or "Everything was in black and white." What they are describing is the effect of stress generated by fear. This fear-generated stress will raise blood pressure and can deplete one's immune system. Fear causes errors in judgment and prevents one from taking the most reasonable course of action. The Bible says, "God is our refuge and strength, a very present help in trouble. Therefore we will not fear" (Psalm 46:1-2). In our text today, we will examine what fear can do and how trusting God can turn a bad situation to good.

There are two women in the Bible who are unknown to most people. The women are Shiphrah (SHIP—raw), which means beautiful, and Puah (POO—aw), which means splendid. Shiphrah and Puah were midwives to the Hebrew women in Egypt. Over 3000 years ago, these women faced fear head on; they made a choice between fear of Pharaoh or faith in God. I am convinced that we either fight fear with faith in God, or it will destroy us. Fear can paralyze us and make our lives unfruitful. Unless we fight fear with faith, we will not be able to grab a hold of the promises that are ours in Jesus Christ. "Because those who are led by the Spirit of God are sons of God. For you did not receive a spirit that makes you a slave again to fear, but you received the Spirit of sonship. And by Him we cry, *'Abba*, Father'" (Romans 8:14-15).

There are two scenes that I want to draw to your attention. The first scene is the new Egyptian Pharaoh, and his initial, ill-timed and ill-fated move to increase severe methods of controlling the Israelites who were enslaved in Egypt during this time in their history. Exodus 1:8 reads, "Then a new king, who did not know about Joseph, came to power in Egypt." New to his position, Pharaoh's insecurity concerning his ability to hold onto control led him to fear the increasing number of Israelites. The Israelites were not only increasing in number, but also in strength; they were becoming a mighty nation. What is important for you to understand is that the increase of the Israelite families came from God's promise to Abraham. God promised to bless Abraham and his offspring. He also promised Abraham that he would become a blessing to all who would bless him. In Genesis 12:2-3, God told Abram (before his name was Abraham), "I will make you into a great nation and I will bless you; I will make your name great, and you will be a blessing. I will bless those who bless you, and whoever curses you I will curse; and all peoples on earth will be blessed through you." This is God's original blessing passed down through generations. This same blessing applies to us today; it was redeemed by the blood of Jesus. By faith, we can have everything that Deuteronomy 28:1-13 describes if we obey the Lord our God and follow His commandments.

Dr. Gloria Ann Turner

The Lord says that all these blessings shall come upon you and overtake you:

1. You will be blessed in the cities. You will be blessed out in the country.
2. Your children will be blessed. Your crops will be blessed. The young animals among your livestock will be blessed. That includes your calves and lambs.
3. Your baskets and bread pans will be blessed.
4. You will be blessed no matter where you go.
5. Enemies will rise up against you. But the Lord will help you win the battle over them. They will come at you from one direction. But they will run away from you in seven directions.
6. The Lord your God will bless your barns with plenty of grain and other food. He will bless everything you do. He will bless you in the land he is giving you.
7. The Lord your God will make you His holy people. He will set you apart for Himself. He took an oath and promised to do that. He promised to do it if you would keep His commands and live exactly as He wants you to live. All of the nations on earth will see that you belong to the Lord. And they will be afraid of you.
8. The Lord will give you more than you need. You will have many children. Your livestock will have many little ones. Your crops will do very well. All of that will happen in the land he promised with an oath to your fathers to give you.

9. The Lord will open up the heavens. That is where He stores His riches. He will send rain on your land at just the right time. He will bless everything you do. You will lend money to many nations. But you won't have to borrow from any of them. The Lord your God will make you leaders, not followers.

You must understand, when God blesses you, no one can do anything about it because YOU ARE BLESSED!

The blessings of the Israelites frightened the new king. He was afraid that the Israelites would one day rise up against him and overtake Egypt. "Come, we must deal shrewdly with them or they will become even more numerous, and if war breaks out, they will join our enemies, fight against us and leave the country" (Exodus 1:10). The new Pharaoh assigned abusive taskmasters to rule over the Israelites. Fear led Pharaoh to do desperate things, and he took evil measures. His solution was to institute more repressive measures of control. The Bible tells us that the more Pharaoh oppressed the Israelites, the more they multiplied. Pharaoh became more fearful and ruthless, deciding to use a harsher method of control: infanticide. He wanted all of the Israelites' baby boys destroyed at birth. This shrewd king wanted to eliminate an entire new generation of people. Clearly, irrational fear was at work.

In the second scene, there is another kind of fear at work. It centers on the two Hebrew midwives whom I have already introduced to you. It is here that we read of the two intriguing, and to my way of thinking, delightful encounters Shiphrah and Puah have with the Pharaoh. I call this kind of fear

"God-fearing" because it reverences God. Hebrews 12:28-29 is a good description of this: "Therefore, since we are receiving a kingdom that cannot be shaken, let us be thankful, and so worship God acceptably with reverence and awe, for our God is a consuming fire." This reverence is exactly what the fear of God means for Christians. This is the motivating factor for us to surrender to the creator of the universe.

In the case of Shiphrah and Puah, the Bibles says, "The midwives, however, feared God and did not do what Pharaoh had told them to do; they let the boys live." They must have had some fear of Pharaoh because of what he could have done to them. However, their rational fear was far out weighted by the trust in God which motivated their behavior. The midwives were God-fearing women; they did what was right in the sight of God. As a result of their trust in God, the boys lived. Whenever you are trusting God to move on your behalf, it will happen because that is what the Bible tells us faith does, it moves mountains. All Christians go through times of difficulty; however, they help us to refocus on God and become more dependent upon Him. During these difficult times, our faith is refined into pure gold. It is time to focus on things that we cannot see with our physical eyes, on things that are spiritual, and use the eyes of our heart. In Hebrews 11: 3, it reads, "By faith we understand that the universe was formed at God's command, so that what is seen was not made out of what was visible."

When Pharaoh confronted Shiphrah and Puah about their disobedience to his decree, they gave him a wonderful, clever response, "Hebrew women are not like Egyptian women, they are vigorous. They give birth before we can get there, and so we can't kill the baby boys instantly when the mothers are on the birth stool as you have commanded." This action by the midwives is the first recorded act of civil disobedience in history. The midwives were motivated by a godly-fear and a trust in God. It is their example that has inspired countless women, such as Harriet Tubman, whose efforts on behalf of runaway slaves became the Underground Railroad, and Rosa Parks, whose refusal to move to the back of the bus sparked the Montgomery Bus Boycott. More recently, we have seen it in mothers and grandmothers who gather in public places demanding to know why their husbands, sons, and grandsons have not been treated equally while serving their country.

If I were to ask you, "What fear is chewing away at you?" Would your answer be an unidentified pain in your body, or maybe an upcoming doctor's appointment and its potential life-threatening results? Is it a relationship gone bad that you desperately want repaired? Is your marriage in trouble? Are your children on drugs or alcohol? Could it be that you are losing your job? Is your teenage daughter pregnant? Are you losing your house or car? Fear can come unexpectedly, but you are not alone. No one lives without fear, but you should not allow fear to control you. It is written in 2 Timothy 1:7, "God did not give us a spirit of fear, but a spirit of power, of love and of self discipline." God made a promise in Isaiah 26:3 that "He will keep you in perfect peace, whose mind is steadfast, because you trust in Him." When you embrace the idea of trusting God when fear comes, the Holy Spirit will overtake that fear and destroy it. God loves us. "There is no fear in love. But perfect love drives out fear, because fear has to do with punishment. The one who fears is not made perfect in love" (1 John 4:18).

When Shiphrah and Puah were commanded by Pharaoh to execute his plan, they had to make a decision. Most people would have done what the king demanded; however, these two brave women disobeyed Pharaoh, placing their own lives in peril because they feared God more. Do not allow fear to break your spirit in trusting God. Remember, we are more than conquerors. If you want to overcome fear, place your faith in Jesus. Jesus will give you the victory! PRAISE THE LORD! AMEN.

LET'S PRAY TOGETHER

Loving Father,

Your love reminds us that we do not need to fear, but can rest in the promises that we inherit as Your children. We pray that we will place our trust in Your Word, rather than the opinions of others. We thank You for our redemption that came through the blood of Jesus Christ. We pray these things in the name of Jesus, our Savior and King, Amen.

Sermon Four

I KNOW A PLACE

"The Shadow of God"
Scripture Reading: Psalm 91:1

He that dwelleth in the secret place of the Most High shall abide under the shadow of the Almighty.

In 1948, a black family gospel group was born called "The Staple Singers." This quartet first appeared in Chicago-area churches. Later on, The Staple Singers began recording secular songs. They were best known for their hits "I'll Take You There," "Respect Yourself," and "Let's Do It Again." In 1972, "I'll Take You There" topped both the Pop and R&B charts, remaining at number one for four weeks. In this song, the lead singer Mavis Staple is inviting her listeners to seek heaven:

> I know a place
> Ain't nobody cryin'
> Ain't nobody worried

Dr. Gloria Ann Turner

> Ain't no smilin' faces
> Lyin' to the races
> Help me, come on, come on
> Somebody, help me now
> I'll take you there, help me, y'all, I'll take you there.

Psalm 91:1 is also an invitation for listeners to seek a special place—a place in heaven. However, the invitation is not for all listeners. The invitation is only for those who believe that Jesus is the Messiah, the Son of God, and the Mighty One in deed and word. Every child of God who lives in close fellowship with Him looks toward the inner sanctuary and the mercy seat of God. Some of God's children run to Him enjoying occasional visits, but they do not habitually reside in His glorious presence. Those who want to reside in the presence of God must commune with Him morning, noon, and night. Daily, saints must abide with Christ, and Christ will abide with them. Saints possess a secret place in God. In other words, they have ownership in Christ. Jesus paid the price for us to have ownership in God's kingdom. Saints are the true lovers of God in Christ Jesus. To them the veil is torn, the mercy seat is revealed, and the glory of God is manifested, over and over again.

Our scripture reading begins with "He that dwelleth." The first word is the pronoun "he." This refers to the one who dwells. That would be YOU! The "he" can be someone rich or poor, educated or uneducated, young or old, male or female, for we know that God loves all persons—for man is His crowning achievement. Certainly, we can gather from the text that the

Living From Faith To Faith

person who dwells with the Lord knows Him. David wrote, "One thing have I desired of the Lord, that will I seek after: that I may dwell in the house of the Lord all the days of my life, to behold the beauty of the Lord, and to inquire in his temple" (Psalm 27:4). David had many enemies and major problems confronting him; nevertheless, he rejoiced at the opportunity to worship the Lord. It was in God's presence that David found shelter and safety; he experienced victory over his enemies, and he sang and made music to the Lord.

The Hebrew word for "dwelleth" is *yashab*, which means to abide continually, remain steadfast, settle down, and enduring with consistency. David said, "Lord I have loved the habitation of thy house, and the place where thine honor dwelleth" (Psalm 26:8). In the New Testament, Jesus proclaimed these powerful words, "He that eateth my flesh, and drinketh my blood, dwelleth in me, and I in Him" (John 6:56). Later Jesus said, "Believe me that I am in the Father, and the Father in me: or else believe me for the very works' sake" (John 14:11). As saints, the Holy Spirit must dwell in you. It is the Holy Spirit that does the work; without Him, you cannot serve God.

The prepositional phrase tells us where you must dwell: in the "secret place." So where is the secret place? In ancient days, the secret place was symbolized by *Yahweh's* earthly tabernacle. It was called the "Holiest of all" (Hebrews 9:3), the Holy of Holies; the place where God and God alone dwelled. The Holy of Holies was a small room that contained the Ark of the Covenant (a gold-covered chest that contained the original stone tablets of the Ten Commandments, a jar of manna, and Aaron's staff that had budded). The top of the chest served as the "atonement cover" (or altar) on which the blood would be sprinkled by the high priest on the Day of Atonement (Exodus 24-25). The glory (shekinah) of the God of Israel dwelt between the two cherubims. "And there I will meet with thee, and I will commune with thee from above the mercy seat, from between the two cherubims which are upon the ark of the testimony, of all things which I will give thee in commandment unto the children of Israel" (Exodus 25:22). The Holy of Holies was the most sacred place on earth for the Jews, and only the high priest could enter. After the birth of Christ, God no longer dwelled in houses and temples that were made with human hands. After the resurrection of Jesus, God provided the saints access to His secret place: the headship of Christ. Christ lives in our hearts, a dwelling place for us to meet Him daily. What does it mean to dwell in that sacred, secret place? It means to have absolute faith in God's Word, in God's plan, and in God's destiny.

The secret place is a refuge from the storms of life in this world. It is a place to run to Abba, Father God. Whenever we are facing crises, like sickness of child, death of a loved one, losing a job or financial hardship, we can run to the secret place in Christ Jesus. Psalm 27:5 declared, "For in the day of trouble He will hide me in His shelter, in the secret place of His tent will He hide me; He will set me high upon a rock." Our heart is God's inhabitance and our inhabitance in God, a place for us to live, to move, and to have our being.

The scriptures inform us that the secret place belongs to the "Most High." The Most High is the creator of Heaven and Earth and all that is in it. The Most High was Jesus Christ in the flesh. The Most High has revealed His glory and exposed His greatness to His children. There is one more fact about the Most High: There is *nothing* higher than He. Did you get that? Nothing and no one is higher than our Father. King David said, "I will praise the Lord according to his righteousness and will sing praise to the name of the Lord Most High" (Psalm 7:17).

The last part of the scripture says: "shall abide under the shadow of the Almighty." Abiding denotes a constant and continuous dwelling of the just within the protection of God. The Hebrew word for "shall abide" is *Nkwlty*, which signifies one shall pass the night. Passing the night denotes security and rest in times of darkness, temptation, and calamity. Abraham passed the night with God when He foretold the affliction of Abraham's descendants in Egypt and their subsequent deliverance (Genesis 15:12-16). God told Abraham, "Fear not, I am thy shield" (Genesis 15:1). God showed Abraham the many stars in the sky and told him his descendents would outnumber them. It is through faith that we abide in Christ Jesus. Jesus said, "Abide in me, and I in you. As the branch cannot bear fruit of itself, except it abide in the vine; no more can ye, except ye abide in me" (John 15:4).

The final phrase of the verse, "under the shadow of the Almighty," implies great nearness to God. We must walk very close to God if we would have His shadow over us. The omnipotent Lord will shield all those who dwell with Him. Saints shall remain under His care. Those who commune with God are safe with Him; no evil can reach them, for the outstretched wings of His power and love cover them from all harm. Several years ago, I was seriously injured in a head-on collision. A drunk driver came on my side of the highway. When the car approached me, immediately, I saw a blanket thrown around me, protecting the upper part of my body. God informed me that the blanket was His shadow, shielding me from death. Thanks be to God that I am under the shadow of the Almighty! I agree with King David, "My shield is God Most High, who saves the upright in heart" (Psalm 7:10). God's protection is all sufficient, and His omnipotence will surely shield His children from all attacks. No shelter can be compared to the shelter of God. The shadow of the Almighty is powerful beyond measure, and those who dwell in His secret place will experience it.

This scripture is considered a blessing. The blessing has a condition and a promise attached to it. Listen closely. The condition is that you must dwell in the secret place, and the promise is that you shall abide under the shadow of the Almighty. The Hebrew word for "the Almighty" is *El Shaddai*. While on the Island of Patmos, the Apostle John heard, "I am Alpha and Omega, the beginning and the ending, saith the Lord, which is, and which was, and which is to come, the Almighty" (Revelation 1:8). The Apostle John declared that "the Almighty" is the only one who can make such a claim because in the beginning was the Word, and the Word was with God, and the Word was God (John 1:1).

The Staple Singers sang, 'I Know a place, Ain't nobody cryin, and Ain't nobody worried.' Saints can sing, "He that dwelleth in the secret place of the Most High shall abide under the shadow of the Almighty!" HALLELUJAH! AMEN.

LET'S PRAY TOGETHER

Everlasting Father,

We acknowledge that You are God, the Almighty, the Creator of this universe. We are thankful for the victory that was won for us on the cross and through the resurrection of our Lord and Savior. We are grateful that we have a dwelling place in Jesus and He has a dwelling place in us. We are well equipped to fight the enemies of this world and to live a victorious life each day. We thank You in the name of Jesus, the Lamb of God who takes away our sins. Amen.

Sermon Five

A CHANGED LIFE

"Father's Love"
Scripture Reading: Luke 15:11-24

Jesus continued: "There was a man who had two sons. The younger one said to his father, 'Father, give me my share of the estate.' So he divided his property between them. Not long after that, the younger son got together all he had, set off for a distant country and there squandered his wealth in wild living. After he had spent everything, there was a severe famine in that whole country, and he began to be in need. So he went and hired himself out to a citizen of that country, who sent him to his fields to feed pigs. He longed to fill his stomach with the pods that the pigs were eating, but no one gave him anything. When he came to his senses, he said, 'How many of my father's hired men have food to spare, and here I am starving to death! I will set out and go back to my father and say to him: Father, I have sinned against heaven and against you.

I am no longer worthy to be called your son; make me like one of your hired men.' So he got up and went to his father. But while he was still a long way off, his father saw him and was filled with compassion for him; he ran to his son, threw his arms around him and kissed him. The son said to him, 'Father, I have sinned against heaven and against you. I am no longer worthy to be called your son.' But the father said to his servants, 'Quick! Bring the best robe and put it on him. Put a ring on his finger and sandals on his feet. Bring the fattened calf and kill it. Let's have a feast and celebrate. For this son of mine was dead and is alive again; he was lost and is found.'"

Today's subject is "A Changed Life." We are in the book of Luke, which is one of the synoptic gospels. Scholars believe Luke was probably a Gentile by birth, well educated in Greek culture, and a physician by profession. Doctor Luke was not privileged to be among the twelve who walked so closely with Jesus; he gathered his information from eyewitnesses. Luke did have the honor of spending most of his time working with Paul on his missionary journeys. Certainly, we are privileged to receive Luke's accurate account of Jesus' life on earth and the lasting impact after his ascension.

Each of the gospel writers had a special theme and special audience. Matthew targeted the Jews, and he often talked with them about Jesus being the Messiah. Mark targeted mainly Gentiles. The Christians suffered much persecution under

Nero, the Roman emperor. Mark encouraged Christians with the knowledge that Jesus also suffered much, and was known as the "Suffering Servant." Luke's audience was the Gentiles. He wanted them to know that Jesus was a compassionate, caring, and loving Savior. He focused on showing them Jesus' humanity. The central theme of Luke's gospel was that Jesus came to seek and to save that which was lost. Jesus' ministry was a universal ministry to men, women, children, the rich, and the poor. Jesus came to seek and to save that person who was lost: anyone who was broken, down-hearted, disenfranchised, in pain or in suffering.

Jesus was more of a teacher than a preacher. The first message Jesus preached was when He came out of the wilderness after His forty days and forty nights of fasting. Jesus preached His opening sermon, using the words of the prophet Isaiah: "And the Spirit of the Lord is upon me because the Lord has anointed me to preach the gospel" (Isaiah 61). Thereafter, Jesus taught more than He preached, and He employed many teaching methods in communicating His principles. He would use history, illustration, discourse, and questioning. Jesus' favorite way of communicating His principles was by parable. A parable is an earthly story with a heavenly meaning. Jesus frequently used parables as a means of illustrating profound, divine truths. If you've been to Sunday school or attend church services, you've heard and read about the parables Jesus taught on lost things. The three most popular are the lost coin, the lost sheep, and the lost son. Today, we will discover the lesson surrounding the lost son.

Jesus begins, "There was a man who had two sons. The younger son said to his father, 'Father, give me my share (inheritance) of the estate.' So the Father divided his property between them." It was not unusual in those days for fathers to give an inheritance to their children at a very young age. In the Old Testament, as soon as the child was born, the father began to store up riches or wealth for his child. According to the Jewish culture, they were to store up riches, and then, they were to divide the portions. Of course, the first son would always receive the birthright, an extra inheritance from his father, along with the family blessing; then, the remaining inheritance would be equally divided between the younger sons. Here we see a father's youngest son asking for his portion of his father's riches. Of course, the younger son wanted his portion in cash or coin. He wanted to take it away with him. If he received land or livestock, he liquidated these assets because the Bible tells us that he wasted his wealth in wild living.

The son was at a crossroad in his life. He had a spirit of independence. He no longer wanted to live under his father's rules and regulations. He felt that he could have a better lifestyle away from his father's house. He wanted his own influence, authority, and power. However, the son failed to recognize that he had everything he needed, and more, in his father's house. Everything that belonged to his father belonged to him! Take a look at the following list of things that he had with his father:

1. In John 14: 2, Jesus says, "In my Father's house are many rooms (mansions); if it were not so, I would have told

you, I am going there to prepare a place for you." The son had a mansion, a place of his own in his father's house.
2. In Philippians 4:7, Paul states, "And the peace of God, which passeth all understanding, shall keep your hearts and minds in Christ Jesus." The father had given his son his perfect peace, a righteous and holy peace that comes from Christ Jesus.
3. Matthew 11:28-30 asserts, "Come unto me, all ye that labor and are heavy laden, and I will give you rest. Take my yoke upon you, and learn of me; for I am meek and lowly in heart: and ye shall find rest unto your souls. For my yoke is easy and my burden is light." The father freed the son from a hard yoke and a heavy burden. In his soul, rest was given to him from the father.
4. 1 Peter 1:23 writes, "For you are born again, not of corruptible seed, but of incorruptible, by the Word of God, which lives and abides in you forever." The father's spirit resided within the son.
5. 2 Peter 1:3 proclaims, "Because God's divine power has given us everything necessary for life and godliness. This power was given to us through the knowledge of the one who has been our guide by his glory and virtue." The son had divine power to live a holy and righteous life; also, he was given knowledge, wisdom, and revelation to live a victorious life.
6. 2 Peter 1:4 declares, "God has given us exceedingly great and precious promises." The son even had a great

blessing—a covenant with his father. What were the great promises?

- "God shall supply all your needs according to his riches in glory by Christ Jesus" (Philippians 4:19).
- "If ye abide in me, and my words abide in you, ye shall ask what ye will, and it shall be done unto you" (John 15:7).
- "But seek ye first the kingdom of God, and His righteousness; and all these things shall be added unto you" (Matthew 6:33).

All of these were blessings the son had in his Father's house. Guess what? These same blessings belong to you and to me. In God's house, we have everything that we need to live a good and abundant life. We have God's Spirit, salvation, peace, rest, prosperity, and power. All of these are given as great promises from God.

The son no longer wanted to submit to his father's will, plan, or purpose. He wanted his own time—he wanted to do his own thing. That is what this boy was asking for: give me my space. The son cried, "Father, you're in my space; I need my own space!" How many of you are telling God that today? *God, I want to make my own choices, and I want to determine my own destiny.* People come to church on Sunday to listen to the Word, but their minds are not focused on the Word. Their bodies are here, but their minds are out there. Some are anxious to leave before the church service ends because they have other things that are more important than the Word. They have already set up their own systems to function outside of the will of God. They have set up ways to justify why they make certain choices. People have set up ways to walk in darkness by tip-toeing here and there. Jesus said that men loved darkness instead of light because their deeds are evil (John 3:19). So what do you do with that kind of mind? You let it go! The Bible says that the father gave his son the inheritance, and his son went into a far country. Why did he travel to a far county? The boy did not want anyone to recognize him, and he wanted to break away from traditions, customs, and memories. He wanted to separate himself from anything that represented his father's views.

The boy left home and associated with the wrong type of people. He was hanging around the clubs late at night, wasting money, wasting time, and wasting purpose. The Bible said that he wasted his substance in wild living without saving a dime. Because of his lifestyle choices, he ran out of money and came to a place of emptiness. Later, the boy took a job feeding pigs. He was so hungry that the pigs' food began to look good to him. He was empty physically, emotionally, and spiritually. Nevertheless, the Bible says, "then he came to his senses." In other words, the boy turned his heart back to his father. He said, "I will set out and go back to my father and say to him: Father, I have sinned against heaven and against you." I believe in that same hour, the boy received a changed heart. His life was miraculously changed!

Drawing near to home, his father recognized him and ran to embrace him with much love and forgiveness. The father called family and friends to celebrate with him the good news of his son returning home. This same thing takes place when you come to Jesus. Jesus receives you with much joy. There is nothing better than experiencing a changed life in Christ Jesus, a life that our God designed for you. PRAISE THE LORD! AMEN.

LET'S PRAY TOGETHER

Heavenly Father,

We come into Your presence with thanksgiving and praise. For we know there is no love greater than Your love for us. We submit to Your Word which is Your will for our lives. We surrender ourselves completely to You and confess total dependence upon You in every area of our lives: spirit, soul and body. We thank You in Jesus' name. Amen.

Sermon Six

TRUE WORSHIPERS

"Reverence God"
Scripture Reading: Matthew 21:10-13

When Jesus entered Jerusalem, the whole city was stirred and asked, "Who is this?" The crowds answered, "This is Jesus, the prophet from Nazareth in Galilee." Jesus entered the temple area and drove out all who were buying and selling there. He overturned the tables of the money changers and the benches of those selling doves. "It is written," he said to them, "My house will be called a house of prayer, but you are making it a den of robbers."

Today, we turn to the Gospel of Matthew. Matthew means "the gift of Jehovah." In the Bible, Matthew is referred to as a "publican" (Mark 2:14, 3:18, and Luke 5:27). There was a time when the word publican was an honorable word, but words have a way of changing through time and culture. In Jesus' time, the word publican was equated with the words thief, hustler, liar, and crook. Matthew was a tax collector, and he worked at the customs office. He was a Jew; however, he was not committed to his people because he collected taxes from them for the Roman government and was not always honest. Oddly enough, Jesus went to the customs office and told Matthew, "Follow me." Matthew became a disciple of Jesus Christ, and he was included in the twelve, along with Peter, James, John, and the others. The Gospel of Matthew begins with the genealogy of Jesus as a way to acknowledge his belief that Jesus was the Messiah, the King of Kings and the Lord of Lords. Jesus came from the lineage of David, out of the tribe of Judah.

This Scripture reading was during the last week of Jesus' life called "Passion Week" on the Christian calendar. Jesus continued to go about his Father's business of establishing the kingdom of God on earth. The kingdom of God has some specific assignments and tasks, one of which was to bring healing to the nation of Israel. Jesus went to the temple with this great proclamation: "The Spirit of the Lord is on me, because he has anointed me to preach good news to the poor. He has sent me to proclaim freedom for the prisoners and recovery of sight for the blind, to release the oppressed, to proclaim the year of the Lord's favor" (Luke 4:18-19). The mission of the church should be exactly the same. Every time we come into the house of God, we should come expecting the impartation and manifestation of God. In other words, God's anointing should be made visible because we are the temple of God and our spirit is one with Him. "God is spirit, and those who worship Him must worship Him in spirit and in truth" (John 4:24). These are the exact words spoken by Jesus to a Samaritan woman at Jacob's well. Jesus said, "Yet a time is coming and has now come when the true worshipers will worship the Father in spirit and truth, for they are the kind of worshipers the Father seeks" (John 4:23).

There was a large crowd following Jesus as He entered Jerusalem during the last week of His life. Throughout Jesus' ministry, the religious authorities were disturbed over the large crowds following Him. Even though the Old Testament prophets had performed the same works, the people were impressed with Jesus' ability to multiply the bread and fish, to heal the sick, and to raise the dead. Rumors were rampant regarding who Jesus was. Was He John the Baptist? Elijah? Jeremiah? Was He one of the prophets? Who was this man? If I were to ask you today, "Who was Jesus?" or rather, would you be able to tell me, "Who is Jesus?" If you do not know, I will tell you—Jesus was God in the flesh! The disciple Thomas declared Him as "My Lord and My God" (John 20:28). Apostle Paul described Him as, ". . . our Great God and Savior, Jesus Christ" (Titus 2:13). The Prophet Isaiah proclaimed Him as, "A Wonderful Counselor, Mighty God, Everlasting Father, and the Prince of Peace" (Isaiah 9:6).

The city was filled with worshipers who had come to celebrate the Passover Feast. When Jesus arrived in Jerusalem, the people gathered palm branches and spread them on the road along with their garments to prepare a royal walkway for Jesus. In Matthew 21:9 the crowds shouted, "Blessed is he who comes in the name of the Lord! Hosanna in the highest!"

In the Book of Zechariah, it was prophesied that Jesus would come as a conquering king: "Rejoice greatly, O daughter of Zion! Shout, O daughter of Jerusalem! Behold, your King is coming to you" (9:9).

At that time, the Jews of the Diaspora were scattered all over the Roman Empire because Rome had conquered Palestine, Egypt, and Syria. All Jews were mandated to come once a year to Jerusalem to celebrate the feast of the Passover, a memorial day to God who passed over the houses of the children of Israel in Egypt when He struck down the Egyptians and delivered the Israelites. As part of the ritual, they were to bring a spotless lamb to the feast of Passover. If they could not afford a lamb, they had to bring a turtledove. Regardless of the animal, blood had to be shed at the ritual. God said, "When I see the blood I will pass over you" (Exodus 12:13).

Jews came from all over and had to exchange their money for Jerusalem's currency to buy animals for this ritual. The outer court of the temple was overflowing with merchants and money changers. The feast of Passover was a sacred ritual and people had to come to God with a sacrifice in their hands. Likewise, we need to come to the Lord's house with something in our hand. We should bring our sacrifice of praise into the house of the Lord as an offering. Also, we ought to bring our tithes and offerings to God's house. Bring it to the Lord's house. Oh, let's praise Him for everything that He has given us. There is nothing that we have that the Lord has not given to us. There is nothing that we have that the Lord did not bless us with. Let's give Him a sacrifice of praise right now. Hallelujah!

When Jesus saw that the temple in Jerusalem had been transformed into a gathering place for moneychangers, he overturned their tables. He denounced this as a defiling of a sacred place and turning it into a "den of thieves." Today, carbon trading presents us with an alarming parallel. If Jesus were to behold a gathering of modern day "moneychangers" plotting to make huge profits from the destruction of God's creation, it would not be difficult to imagine him calling this an abomination, disrupting the proceeding, and overturning the tables. As the traders scattered, one might hear words such as these: "Woe to those who call evil good, and good evil; who put darkness for light, and light for darkness" (Isaiah 5:20). Listen, I want you to get this: It was not the transaction of the business that offended Jesus; it was the cheating, the greediness, the manipulation, and the sinful spirit in the place. People exchanged money to purchase animals for the needed sacrifice to celebrate the Passover with the shedding of blood. However, the merchants and the money exchangers were manipulating the people at a time when they were coming to worship God. They overcharged for an animal, or cheated them by not giving the proper change. When Jesus saw the dishonesty, the Bible says that something rose up inside of Him. Jesus was angry because there was not a spirit of worship in the place, but a spirit of carnality.

Even today, people come to church for their own agenda, trying to network. They pass out their cards to promote their businesses instead of glorifying and worshipping the Lord. When you come to God's house, you should, "Enter his gates with thanksgiving and his courts with praise; give thanks to

Him and praise his name!" (Psalm 100:4). This is the reason why you should come to a church, to praise and seek the Word of the Lord. As believers, we need the Word of God fed to us daily. The house of God is not for self-glorification; leave your personal agenda at home. There is only one agenda in God's house, and it is the Holy Spirit's agenda to bring truth, to bring healing, and to bring deliverance. Let's praise the Lord for His agenda. Hallelujah!

The Bible says that when Jesus saw the foul spirit of defilement, of manipulation, of corruption, the power of God inside of Him took action. Unfortunately, there are only a few Christians who are willing to take action against ungodliness and unrighteousness in our society. Thank God for Jesus who came to show us the right way. Every now and then we need to put our foot down in order to stay with God's agenda. God wants people's souls to be saved, their lives to be delivered, and their bodies to be healed. God wants people to have a true heart for worship. God told Pharaoh, "Let my people go that they may worship me" (Exodus 8:1). Jesus rebuked Satan, "For it is written, Worship the Lord your God, and serve Him only" (Matthew 4:10). God needs some true worshipers. Will you worship God in spirit and truth today?

Jesus rose up, turned over the tables, took the cord from around His waist, and showed that He was in charge. Jesus put his Father's house in order. Every now and then we must set God's house in order. Jesus made it clear that his Father's house was a house of prayer. The church is not a place for gossiping, lusting, and stealing. One should come to the church to receive understanding of the Word of God and to enjoy corporate worship. We must be taught by the Spirit of God to worship Him. Only the Lord knows how He wants to be worshiped.

1 Kings 18:25-40 contains a story about Elijah standing against the worshipers of Baal. Elijah called the Israelites to a meeting, and asked them, "How long will you waver between two opinions? If the Lord is your God, then you must worship Him. If Baal is your God, then you should worship him." The Bible teaches us that we cannot serve two masters. Luke 16:13 states, "Either he will hate the one and love the other, or he will be devoted to the one and despise the other." Our hearts belong to the Lord, for He created us in His image to worship Him. True worshipers keep a praise at all times for the Lord. True worshipers praise God in spirit and in truth. PRAISE THE LORD! AMEN.

LET'S PRAY TOGETHER

Gracious Father,

Give us a heart to seek an intimate relationship with You every day. Teach us how to worship You with our total being. You created us to glorify, to worship, and to praise You. Help us to follow Your thoughts and ways rather than our own. Thank You for Jesus who taught us how to truly walk with You in good times and in difficult times. We pray this in the name of Jesus, the Author and Finisher of our faith. Amen.

Sermon Seven

STAY FOCUSED

"Prayer Under Trial"
Scripture Reading: Matthew 26:36-46

Then Jesus went with his disciples to a place called Gethsemane, and he said to them, "Sit here while I go over there and pray." He took Peter and the two sons of Zebedee along with him, and he began to be sorrowful and troubled. Then he said to them, "My soul is overwhelmed with sorrow to the point of death. Stay here and keep watch with me." Going a little farther, he fell with his face to the ground and prayed, "My Father, if it is possible, may this cup be taken from me. Yet not as I will, but as you will." Then he returned to his disciples and found them sleeping. "Could you men not keep watch with me for one hour?" he asked Peter. "Watch and pray so that you will not fall into temptation. The spirit is willing, but the body is weak." He went away a second time and prayed, "My Father, if it is not possible for this cup to be taken away unless

> *I drink it, may your will be done." When he came back, he again found them sleeping, because their eyes were heavy. So he left them and went away once more and prayed the third time, saying the same thing. Then he returned to the disciples and said to them, "Are you still sleeping and resting? Look, the hour is near, and the Son of Man is betrayed into the hands of sinners. Rise, let us go! Here comes my betrayer!"*

In this text, we read about Jesus facing death head on, suffering as the Redeemer of His people. The Jesus we find in the Garden of Gethsemane is not the same Jesus we read much about early in the scriptures. Jesus healed those who were blind, paralyzed, lame, crippled, and plagued with various illnesses. He fed 5,000 people with only five loaves of bread and two fish, changed the water into wine, and raised people from the dead. But our Lord Jesus in this text is distressed, troubled, and deeply grieved. The Garden of Gethsemane frequently served as a quiet place of peaceful reflection and of intimate fellowship with His Heavenly Father. Luke 22:39 implies that Jesus went as a frequent visitor to this garden on the side of the Mount of Olives. He also had the presence of His disciples whenever He visited that garden. However, the last time our Lord visited Gethsemane, it was the furthest thing from a place of peace and refreshing renewal. Rather, it was a place of lonely agony, grief, and abandonment by both His human companions and His Heavenly Father.

Living From Faith To Faith

All three synoptic gospels (Matthew, Mark, and Luke) give us a detailed account of Christ's agony in the Garden of Olives, known in Hebrew as "Gethsemane." Gethsemane was possibly a remote walled garden. The Gospels Mark and Matthew describe Gethsemane as being located near the Mount of Olives. The Gospel of John describes Jesus' betrayal as occurring in a garden, outside the city, located across the Kidron Valley, east of Jerusalem, and near the western slope of the Mount of Olives. John also tells us this was a place where Jesus often went with his disciples.

There is a contrast between the Garden of Eden and the Garden of Gethsemane. In the first garden, the Garden of Eden, the first man Adam fell by yielding to temptation. In the second garden, the Garden of Gethsemane, the second man Jesus conquered by yielding to the will of God. Gethsemane was a place of victory for Jesus and consequently for us as well. But the victory did not come easily. It came with a price.

Jesus told His disciples that He was deeply distressed, "even to death," and asked Peter, James, and John to wait at a certain place while He went ahead to pray. Jesus was asking the three disciples to stay focused and keep watch because the situation that was about to take place would be a most memorable one during their ministry. Jesus went a little farther on the path, fell to the ground, and prayed to His Father. Jesus requested to be relieved from His suffering; yet, He made it clear that He would do what God the Father commanded. He returned to Peter, James, and John and found them asleep. Jesus was disappointed that they were not even able to stay awake as He underwent such agony. It was the hardest time for Jesus.

Dr. Gloria Ann Turner

He really desired His disciples to stay focused with Him at that time. If you can recall, these three disciples had special pledges. They were with Jesus at one of His greatest miracles—raising a little girl from the dead. They also saw Jesus transfigured on the mountainside. At that moment, Jesus returned to find them sleeping during a time when He desired fellowship and comfort. Gethsemane was not only a geographical location, but it was also a place of suffering and pain. On our Christian journey, we will experience Gethsemanes, places of tragedy, disaster, and intense sorrow. When a Gethsemane comes—and believe me, it will come—don't lose hope, don't stop trusting, and don't give up. It is important to stay focused on the Word of God when you are going through difficult times. You must remember to meditate on the scriptures, which contain the following promises:

- "Be anxious for nothing, but in everything by prayer and supplication, with thanksgiving, let your requests be made known to God: and the peace of God, which surpasses all understanding; will guard your hearts and minds through Christ Jesus" (Philippians 4:6-7).
- "These things I have spoken unto you, that in me ye might have peace. In the world ye shall have tribulation: but be of good cheer; I have overcome the world" (John 16:33).
- "Come unto me, all ye that labor and are heavy laden, and I will give you rest. Take my yoke upon you, and learn of me; for I am meek and lowly in heart: and ye

shall find rest unto your souls. For my yoke is easy, and my burden is light" (Matthew 11:28-30).
- "But my God shall supply all your needs according to his riches in glory by Christ Jesus" (Philippians 4:19).
- "Whereby are given unto us exceeding great and precious promises: that by these ye might be partakers of the divine nature, having escaped the corruption that is in the world through lust" (2 Peter 1:4).
- "Blessed is the man that walketh not in the counsel of the ungodly, nor standeth in the way of sinners, nor sitteth in the seat of the scornful. But his delight is in the law of the LORD; and in his law doth he meditate day and night. And he shall be like a tree planted by the rivers of water, that bringeth forth his fruit in his season; his leaf also shall not wither; and whatsoever he doeth shall prosper" (Psalm 1:1-3).

The Word of God must be alive and active in us. When we read the Bible, we're not just reading a book, we're reading the sacred Word of God. The Bible contains the very Words of God, and it is given to us that we might know Him, love Him, and obey Him. It is imperative to know that we simply cannot understand the Bible apart from the enlightening power of God's Spirit. We must have God open our eyes to understand and apply the glorious truths that we read in scripture. Apart from the Spirit of God, our devotional times would be dry, lifeless, and fruitless. Before you read God's Word, pray that God would give you understanding.

In the Garden of Gethsemane, words of agony were heard in Jesus' prayer: "Father, if it is possible, let this cup pass from Me. Not as I will, but as You will. If this cup cannot pass away from Me unless I drink it, Your will be done." In other words, Jesus indicated that if this cup of suffering could not be removed, then He desired the Father's strength to drink it. There will be times in our lives that God might not move the mountain or the things that are hindering us, but God will give us the strength to make it through and endure. We will get the victory and see the glory of God if we faint not. Praise the Lord!

Three times Jesus found the disciples sleeping instead of watching and praying. He scolded His disciples for failing to stay focused. "Could you men not keep watch with me for one hour?" He said. He shared with the disciples that it was a difficult hour for Him, "My spirit is willing, but the flesh is weak." Jesus knew that God had the power to do all things. He trusted His Father, even though He knew that sin was separating Him from God. In 2 Corinthians 5:21, Paul wrote, "God made Him who had no sin to be sin for us," and in Galatians 3:13 he wrote, "Christ redeemed us from the curse of the law by becoming a curse for us."

Jesus stayed focused on His purpose and His destiny, saying, "The one who sent me is with me; he has not left me alone, for I always do what pleases Him" (John 8:29). An important factor for us to understand is that the Lord's suffering in Gethsemane was in His obedient surrender to the Father's will. No form of resistance was possible. Jesus was being led like a lamb to the slaughter. Because of His obedience, God turned that garden of suffering into a garden of strength. God strengthened Jesus with His power. "But they that wait upon the Lord shall renew their strength; they shall mount up with wings as eagles; they shall run, and not be weary; and they shall walk, and not faint" (Isaiah 40:31). God will do the same for us when we surrender our lives to Him and are obedient. It does not matter what you are going through; your faith in the Lord Jesus will strengthen you through hard and difficult times. We must stay focused on what the Word of God promises us and expect victorious results. Know this for sure, "I can do all things through Christ who strengthens me" (Philippians 4:13). PRAISE THE LORD! AMEN.

LET'S PRAY TOGETHER

Sovereign Father,

We come to You in the name of Jesus, acknowledging You as our Refuge and Strength. You are our Stronghold in times of trouble. By faith, we respond to trouble with patience and confidence knowing that we are more than conquerors. Instead of worrying, we will pray. We will let our petitions turn our prayers into perfect praise. We thank You in Jesus' name. Amen.

Sermon Eight
DOES GOD SHOW FAVORITISM?

"Judging"
Scripture Reading: Acts 10:9-16

About noon the following day as they were on their journey and approaching the city, Peter went up on the roof to pray. He became hungry and wanted something to eat, and while the meal was being prepared, he fell into a trance. He saw heaven opened and something like a large sheet being let down to earth by its four corners. It contained all kinds of four-footed animals, as well as reptiles of the earth and birds of the air. Then a voice told him, "Get up, Peter. Kill and eat." "Surely not, Lord!" Peter replied. "I have never eaten anything impure or unclean." The voice spoke to him a second time, "Do not call anything impure that God has made clean." This happened three times, and immediately the sheet was taken back to heaven.

Dr. Gloria Ann Turner

Recently, I visited Los Angeles, California, for the first time. As I was driving down the street, I was amazed how one side of the street—where the big, luxury homes were located—the street signs were made with expensive materials, such as handcrafted, gold metal letters. However, on the opposite side of the same street—where the smaller, inexpensive homes were located—the street signs were made with cheap materials, such as pine wood, painted with blue and white letters. We live in a world in which we constantly build boundaries. In our neighborhoods, we want to separate ourselves, stand out among average people. We yearn for more individuality as we try to define who we are in clubs, fraternities, sororities, racial/ethnic groups, and most of them are based on political affiliations and gender preferences. For some reason, being God's beloved child isn't enough. Our efforts at individuality make us feel better, and in so doing, we deny the reality of the universal love of our Creator. The motive behind our attempts to establish individuality within artificial boundaries is a frightened claim on some sense of security in a very insecure world. We look for something artificial to hold onto in a world that is constantly changing and frequently violent. Ultimately, all of our attempts at this false security will be useless. Our only place, our only security, is found in God and in the unity of all of God's people. You are God's precious creation!

Our Scripture setting begins with Peter up on the roof of a house in the city of Joppa. While praying on the rooftop, he has a vision of a large sheet being lowered to the earth. In the sheet, there are all kinds of creatures, reptiles, and birds. Then the Lord spoke to Peter saying, "Get up, Peter; kill and eat." But

Peter says, "By no means, Lord; I have never eaten anything that is profane or unclean." The Lord replies, "What God has made clean, you must not call profane." This experience happened three times. While Peter tries to come to an understanding of his vision, messengers from Cornelius arrive at the house and invite Peter to come with them. The Holy Spirit told Peter to go with them without hesitation. When Peter arrives at Cornelius' house, he finds a room full of Cornelius' relatives and close friends. Peter, who is shocked at the reception, says, "You know that it is unlawful for a Jew to associate with or to visit a Gentile; however, God has shown me that I should not call anyone profane or unclean." Then Peter proclaims, "I now realize how true it is that God does not show favoritism but accepts men from every nation who fear Him and do what is right." During Peter's discourse, the Holy Spirit fell on the Gentiles; the Holy Spirit came upon them the same way the Jews received the Holy Spirit on the day of Pentecost. Afterwards, Peter baptized with water the entire house of Cornelius in the name of Jesus Christ.

Peter's sermon opens with a strong statement: God shows no favoritism. Praise the Lord, God shows no partiality! God does not value one person, or church group, or race more than any other. Peter converses that God accepts anyone who fears Him and does what is right in His sight. God wants His children to pursue justice, righteousness, and humility. Peter told the disciples that even though they had been appointed by Jesus to proclaim His good news, they were not "the special group." More importantly, the message of God's salvation and the presence of God's love were not meant solely for the nation of

Israel, but for all people. To Peter that meant God's grace was not limited to just one group of people. Ephesians 2:8-10 tells us, "For it is by grace you have been saved, through faith—and this not from yourselves, it is the gift of God—not by works, so that no one can boast. For we are God's workmanship, created in Christ Jesus to do good works, which God prepared in advance for us to do." Those who are outside the boundaries, those who are trying so hard to fulfill their own destiny, are all included in the grasp of God's love and mercy. Jesus came to save not a few select Jews, but everyone, Gentiles included. Jesus came not for one race, but all races. Jesus came not for one economic class or political party, but for everyone. We often have trouble seeing God's love for others who are beyond the boundaries of our choices and groups. The problem is that people find it difficult not to believe that God must be at least a little partial to them. We have it somewhere hidden in our minds that surely God likes us the best.

Part of our human sinfulness is that we are guilty of making judgments about other people. We are so quick to judge people based on their looks, speech, dress, money, profession, credentials, etc. Personally, one of my favorite passages is when Jesus says, "Do not judge, so that you may not be judged. For with the measure you give, the measure you will get. Why do you see the speck that is in your neighbor's eye, but do not notice the log in your own eye. Or how can you say to your neighbor, 'Let me take the speck out of your eye, while the log is in your own eye?'" (Matthew 7:1-5) Judging, as Jesus condemned it in these verses, is unforgiving condemnation—a hypercritical, self-righteous, vindictive spirit that continually seeks to uncover the faults of others while overlooking one's own sins.

Unfortunately, there was a constant battle for Peter who tried to fight the bias, prejudice, and bigotry in people. Peter's explanation was that God sees everyone alike because He sees everyone through Jesus. That's awesome! That was the purpose of the incarnation of God in human flesh. "The Word became flesh and made his dwelling among us. We have seen his glory, the glory of the One and Only who came from the Father, full of grace and truth" (John 1:14). Paul wanted the believers to get a better understanding of Jesus' purposes and how He sees us.

The early church fathers also pursued this theme of God's inclusiveness that goes beyond all of the boundaries that we create to exclude those we do not like. When we look at Peter's sermon, we need to remember that in the earliest days of Christianity, God was encouraging the enormous implications of the incarnation which we have made more and more restrictive as time has gone on. God's love extends to those who are outside the boundaries of our particular beliefs, regardless of whether those boundaries concern religious, social or political beliefs. The truth is that "For anyone who does not love his brother, whom he has seen, cannot love God, whom he has not seen. And he has given us this command: Whoever loves God must also love his brother" (1 John 4:20-21).

Many Biblical scholars have observed that the Wise Men, who came from different races and cultures representing a wide variety of social, political, and personal morals, were the earliest vindication of the old saying: "If God is not Lord of all, then God is not Lord at all." If we cannot see God in the stranger, in the faces of those whom we cannot understand, in the faces of our enemies, then we will soon lose the ability to see the Creator. We must find God even in our enemy, or we will soon lose sight of God in others. Christianity is not a simple system of rules and regulations. Christianity is Christ alive in all of us, uniting us, healing us, perfecting us through His universal love because not one of us needs God's love and mercy any less than the other. We must stop trying to define ourselves as better as or less sinful than anyone else. When we come to God with the humble recognition that Christ's birth, baptism, death, and resurrection are needed by us all equally, we are able to see that blocking anyone else's access to God and denying our equality with them in the presence of God is denying the truth of the incarnation and placing limits on God's love. Most frightening of all is to deny the boundlessness of Christ's sacrifice.

The whole Christian gospel could be summed up in this point: when God reaches for His children, He is telling us the same thing that He told Jesus that we are His beloved (Matthew 3:17). He sees us not as we are in ourselves, but as we are in Jesus Christ. It sometimes seems impossible, especially to people who have never had this kind of support from their earthly parents; however, it is true that you are His dear child, and He delights in you. Try reading that sentence slowly with your own name; quietly, reflect on God speaking that to you daily. God loved you before you even knew you needed love! "In this was manifested the love of God toward us, because that God sent His only begotten Son into the world, that we might live through Him" (1 John 4:9). He did this by revealing Himself to us as love, a Beloved Father sending his Beloved Son to us. Through the Beloved Son, we come to know ourselves as begotten of God and begotten of His love. As Jesus taught His disciples, we should demonstrate the desire to love one another and the power of love to heal one another. By loving, we will know God, Jesus, and the Holy Spirit as love. Why doesn't the reality of God's love sink in? Why do we hear about it, maybe even find it hard to understand, but once we do understand, forget about it almost immediately and go on with our everyday lives? Jesus taught about God's tender love for us in so many ways—through parables, signs, and other teachings, and most importantly by His example. Yet, when all this was being consummated in Jesus' Passion, almost all of His disciples ran away and believed Him to be dead. When Jesus rose, many were still slow to believe in Him.

We are called to a deep intimacy with God and to love one another. "A new commandment I give unto you, That ye love one another; as I have loved you, that ye also love one another" (John 13:34). God does not call merely a few, but each one of us to love. If we turn to Him and stay long enough to listen, we will never be able to lament that God never answers our prayers. We will know His answer, if not in words, in His perfect peace that passes all understanding that only the Holy Spirit can give. When we do not know how to pray, the Holy Spirit prays for us, and we truly know then that it is HE who loved us first, who is always there listening, loving, and waiting for us. PRAISE THE LORD! AMEN.

Dr. Gloria Ann Turner

LET'S PRAY TOGETHER

Loving Father,

 We thank You that Your love has been poured forth into our hearts by the Holy Spirit. We are committed to walk in Your love and to see Christ in others. We repent for being envious, jealous or cruel to our brothers and sisters. Everywhere we go, we will be committed to plant seeds of love. We know that the seeds will produce Your love in the hearts to whom they are given. For Your Word tells us that we are all one in the body of Christ, in Jesus' precious name. Amen.

Sermon Nine

EXERCISE YOUR FAITH

"Power of God"
Scripture Reading: Hebrews 11:23-29

By faith Moses' parents hid him for three months after he was born, because they saw he was no ordinary child, and they were not afraid of the king's edict. By faith Moses, when he had grown up, refused to be known as the son of Pharaoh's daughter. He chose to be mistreated along with the people of God rather than to enjoy the pleasures of sin for a short time. He regarded disgrace for the sake of Christ as of greater value than the treasures of Egypt, because he was looking ahead to his reward. By faith Moses left Egypt, not fearing the king's anger; he persevered because he saw him who is invisible. By faith he kept the Passover and the sprinkling of blood, so that the destroyer of the firstborn would not touch the firstborn of Israel. By faith the people passed through the Red Sea as on dry land; but when the Egyptians tried to do so, they were drowned.

Chapter eleven of Hebrews is often referred to as the faith chapter much like 1 Corinthians 13 is called the love chapter. Hebrews 11 is a grand gallery of faith, and it invites us to pay tribute to many Old Testament heroes of faith such as Noah, Abraham, Sarah, Joseph, and Moses. These men and women were strong in faith, and out of their faith came the strength to endure suffering, the will to obey God's commands, a hope of the coming Messiah, and patience for a godly kingdom. "All these people were still living by faith when they died. They did not receive the things promised; they only saw them and welcomed them from a distance. And they admitted that they were aliens and strangers on earth" (Hebrews 11:13).

It is important to exercise our faith in every circumstance because we live a new lifestyle by faith. "I have been crucified with Christ; it is no longer I who live, but Christ lives in me; and the life which I now live in the flesh I live by faith in the Son of God, who loved me and gave Himself for me" (Galatians 2:20). Faith is the essence of the Christian walk and unless we learn how to apply it in our daily lives, we will not grow in it as God desires. Hebrews 11:1 tells us what faith is: "Faith is the substance of things hoped for, the evidence of things not seen." Most of the discourse that I have heard on faith has been powerful. Apostle Frederick K. C. Price, Founder of Crenshaw Christian Center in California, says, "Faith is acting on the Word of God." Dr. Creflo Dollar, Pastor of World Changers Church International in Georgia and New York, states, "Faith is a practical expression of your confidence in God and His Word." And Dr. Leroy Thompson, Pastor of Word of Life Christian Center in Louisiana, articulates, "Faith is a spiritual force drawing from the living Word to produce living proof." I believe to have faith is to believe God's Word *before* it comes to pass; faith is conviction of truth without tangible proof.

Daily, we all exercise faith in some form or another. When you put money in the bank, by faith you believe that you can draw it out anytime. When you eat at a restaurant, by faith you trust that the meal will be delicious and it won't make you ill. And when you fly, by faith you believe that the pilot knows how to fly the airplane, and he will take you safely to your destination. However, the Christian faith is not about money in a bank, it's not about meals in a restaurant, and it's not about a pilot knowing how to fly an airplane. The Christian faith, God's kind of faith, is complete trust, dependence, confidence, and reliance on the power of God's Holy Spirit revealed through Jesus Christ. Faith must have an object, and the proper object of genuine faith is God. The scripture says, "By grace are ye saved, through faith" (Ephesians 2:8). By faith, we understand that the universe was formed by the Word of God, so what is seen was made from things that were not seen. God spoke things of the world into existence. In Genesis 1:1-4, it reads, "In the beginning God created the heavens and the earth. Now the earth was formless and empty, darkness was over the surface of the deep, and the Spirit of God was hovering over the waters. And God said, 'Let there be light,' and there was light. God saw that the light was good, and he separated the light from the darkness." What I like about God is that He is still separating light from the darkness. As soon as you accept Jesus Christ into your life, you are pulled out of darkness and placed into His light because God is light. He is the same God who removes the darkness (sin) from us. He commands the light, His light, to shine in us, and by faith we must believe that we are children of light.

An atheist also has faith, although he denies the existence of God or any other deities. His views are based solely on what can be found to be true using the scientific method. An atheist concludes that God doesn't exist because God cannot be proven in science. He believes that our universe came into existence from some type of cosmic explosion that hurled matter from several directions, better known as the Big Bang Theory. For him, the earth was formed without the word of a Creator, or any help of a God. But we know by the Word of God and through the power of the Holy Spirit, this world would not exist without a Creator. By faith, we believe that it was God, no one but God.

Hebrews shows us by numerous examples what true faith is. By contrast, it also shows us what faith is not. We see faith doing things that are not possible with humanity. You must understand that both the power of faith and its strength lie in the Lord Jesus Christ, who lives and moves, and where the Spirit dwells within us. When we believe and trust God to do the work of the kingdom, it is Christ who does the work through us. Apostle Paul stated it clearly, "I have been crucified with Christ and I no longer live, but Christ lives in me. The life I live in the body, I live by faith in the Son of God, who loved me and gave himself for me" (Galatians 2:20).

Habakkuk 2:4 says, "Behold the proud, his soul is not upright in him; but the just shall live by his faith." What does it mean to have "faith" from a Hebraic perspective? In our western minds, faith is a mental exercise in knowing that someone or something exists or will act. For instance, if we say "I have faith in God" we are saying "I know that God exists and does what He says He will do." The Hebrew word for faith is *emunah*, an action oriented word meaning "support." This is significant because it is opposite from the western concept of faith, which places the responsibility for action on the object of one's faith. *Emunah* places the responsibility for action on the believer. It is not knowing that God will act, but rather that I will do what I can to support God. This idea of faithful support can be seen in Exodus 17:12, "When Moses' hands grew tired, they took a stone and put it under him, and he sat on it. Aaron and Hur held his hands up—one on one side, one on the other—so his hands remained steady till sunset." It is the *emunah* of Aaron and Hur that held Moses' arms, not the faith of Moses. When someone says "I have faith in God," he or she should be thinking, "I will do what I can to support God."

Faith is a gift from God. "For by the grace given me I say to every one of you: Do not think of yourself more highly than you ought, but rather think of yourself with sober judgment, in accordance with the measure of faith God has given you" (Romans 12:3). This blessed gift of faith can operate on both an individual and corporate level. When God's people come together by faith, they can perform great works; their faith can turn a nation upside down. James 2:17 proclaimed, "In the same way faith by itself, if it is not accompanied by action is dead." Faith in Christ enables us to overcome impossible difficulties and endure trials and tribulation. Faith can open doors that no man can shut.

In Luke 17:5, the disciples said to the Lord, "Increase our faith!" They lived with Jesus for over three years. They saw Him cast out demons, heal the sick, and raise the dead; yet, they still asked Him, "Increase our faith!" Jesus' answer is wonderful. He replied, "If you have faith as small as a mustard seed, you can say to this mountain, 'Move from here to there' and it will move. Nothing will be impossible for you" (Matthew 17:20). Faith grows as the Word is taken into our lives and acted upon. Romans 10:17 says, "So then faith comes from hearing and hearing by the Word of God."

By faith, the Israelites passed through the Red Sea as on dry land, but when the Egyptians tried to do so by their own strength, they drowned. The Israelites passed through safely because they saw the mighty power of God. When we try to do something without God and we do not ask for His guidance, we are setting ourselves up to fail. It is time to stop living without God. God needs to be in everything we do. You and I cannot do things in our own strength. We operate by the power of the living Spirit of God in us.

God designed us to communicate in the language of faith. It is written in 2 Corinthians 4:13, "I believed; therefore I have spoken. With that same spirit of faith we also believe and therefore speak." There is no other way for us to live. It is faith in Christ that will enable us to overcome trials, overcome troubles, and overcome difficult situations that can utterly destroy us. James 1:3 tells us that the "testing of our faith develops perseverance." When you place your faith in God, faith will not fail. Faith in God will work every time! Take a look at these evidences of faith:

Living From Faith To Faith

- By faith, Abel offered to God a more acceptable sacrifice than Cain (Gen. 4:2-5).
- By faith, Enoch was taken by God in a whirlwind and never saw death (Gen. 5:24).
- By faith, Noah obeyed God and built an ark to save himself and his family (Gen. 6:14-9:17).
- By faith, Abraham believed God and it was credited to him as righteousness (Rom. 4:3).
- By faith, a woman with an issue of blood for twelve years was healed (Matt. 9:20-22).
- By faith, the sight of two blind men were restored (Matt. 9:27-30).
- By faith, Jairus' daughter was resuscitated to life (Mark 5:40-42).

Jesus said, "According to your faith will it be done for you." No doubt that the scriptures show that faith plays a key role in receiving from God. Jesus always credited their faith with being the catalyst. God has given us a measure of faith, but it is up to us to exercise it to grow. Romans 1:17 informs us, "For the righteousness of God is revealed from faith to faith, as it is written, The just shall live by faith." Our day-to-day lives are to consist of walking in faith. In order for us to grow in faith, it must be exercised on a regular basis. We need to look at the many things that we are involved in daily and the problems that we come up against as opportunities to exercise our faith. God honors faith! PRAISE THE LORD! AMEN.

Dr. Gloria Ann Turner

LET'S PRAY TOGETHER

Gracious Father,

You have taught us that when we pray, we are to bring others' needs before You. We pray that You will strengthen our faith and the faith of others that have accepted Jesus Christ as their Lord and Savior. We pray that You will empower us and others to pray through each situation until we see victory over all opposition. Thank You for always being there with us and working things out in our favor. In the precious name of Jesus. Amen.

Sermon Ten

THE GLORY OF SEEKING JESUS

"Knowing the Lord"
Scripture Reading: John 12:20-22

> Now there were some Greeks among those who went up to worship at the Feast. They came to Philip, who was from Bethsaida in Galilee, with a request. "Sir," they said, "we would like to see Jesus." Philip went to tell Andrew; Andrew and Philip in turn told Jesus.

There is something glorious about seeking Jesus. I wake up each morning anticipating what new insight I will receive from the Holy Spirit as I read or listen to God's Word. The spirit of expectation must be present when you are seeking Jesus in order to receive a blessing. We have people today who go to church, not to seek Jesus or to worship Him, but to be entertained. They want to see an extraordinary individual onstage. That is one of the problems I see not only with the mega church movement, but also with much of traditional church worship these days. Worship is supposed to be about God's people glorifying Him; instead it has become a theatrical production performed by professionals. Today, I want you to forget about everything—all personal problems and relationships—and only focus on seeking Jesus. Whenever people come to seek Jesus, something glorious happens in their midst.

Our scripture lesson is taken from the Gospel according to John. I love the Gospel of John. It is not one of the synoptic gospels like Matthew, Mark, and Luke. The Gospel of John is in a distinctive class by itself. This particular gospel is considered the most spiritual of all the gospels. John spends time giving us details, signs, and miracles to show that Jesus had divine power. In chapter eleven, we read of Jesus weeping as a man; yet, He raised Lazarus as God. John gives us strong images of Jesus being divine, Jesus being supernatural, and Jesus being the God-man. Our theme is found in John 20:30-31, "And many other signs truly did Jesus in the presence of his disciples, which are not written in this book. But these are written that ye might believe that Jesus is the Christ, the Son of God, and that believing ye might have life through his name."

This particular text is centered on the time after Jesus' triumphant entry into Jerusalem. Sinners and saints recognized that He was not just an ordinary man, that He was the King of Kings and Lord of Lords. Many of the miracles that Jesus performed pushed the Pharisees and chief priests to recognize Him and to accept the fact that they could not stop Him. When the people saw Jesus they shouted, "Hosanna! Blessed is he who comes in the name of the Lord! Blessed be the King of Israel!"

Living From Faith To Faith

These words angered the Pharisees. They had been trying to dishonor Jesus for two and a half years. They were furious because it seemed as if the whole nation followed Him. But you must understand that the people's response was appropriate for the Creator. Why shouldn't creation respond to its Creator? Jesus was with God and the Holy Spirit during creation. "In the beginning was the Word and the Word was with God and the Word was God. He was with God in the beginning. Through Him all things were made; without Him nothing was made that has been made" (John 1:1-3). Creation marks the absolute beginning of a temporal and material world.

The Pharisees and the Jewish leaders were very upset because they could not control the opinions of the people. Only a week earlier, Jesus had raised Lazarus from the dead. Jesus, through the mighty power of God the Father, called Lazarus to come forth after being in the grave for four days. Lazarus was making his appearance with Jesus, testifying that Jesus really was the Christ, the Son of the living God. The Bible tells us that people were rushing to see Him. This event took place during the Passover, when people came to Jerusalem from all over. Jesus always chose times when there were large crowds around to reveal His supernatural abilities. He demonstrated His authority around those who did not like Him and who doubted Him. "And Jesus went about all the cities and villages, teaching in their synagogues, and preaching the gospel of the kingdom, and healing every sickness and every disease among the people" (Matthew 9:35).

Jesus was surrounded by crowds, preventing the Pharisees from arresting Him. The people pressed close to hear what He was saying. Others wished He would perform a healing, so they were attempting to push through the crowd to get close to Him, hoping to get His attention. Among the Jewish pilgrims were Greeks who had come to Jerusalem to worship during Passover. While there, they heard about all that Jesus had been doing. They probably heard about Jesus healing the man born blind (John 9:1-41), healing the nobleman's son (John 4:46-54), or healing the paralytic at Bethesda on the Sabbath (John 5:2-18). They must have wondered if Jesus was the Messiah that they had been seeking. Most of all, they wanted to hear from Jesus directly concerning the kind of relationship that they might have with Him, since they were Greeks. To obtain the answers to their questions, they would have had to arrange to talk privately with Jesus. They must have taken note of the fact that both Philip and Andrew had Greek names. John makes a point of telling us that Philip was from Bethsaida in Galilee. Of all the disciples, Philip appeared to be the most likely to be inclined to lend a sympathetic ear to Greeks. And so they approached him, requesting to meet with Jesus. Philip wasn't quite sure how to handle this request, so he consulted with Andrew. The two of them would have then pressed their way through the crowd in order to get to the Lord. I can see Philip standing by the Lord as He taught, and at an opportune moment, caught Jesus' attention, whispering in His ear, "There are some Greeks here who would like to talk with You." Most scholars conclude that these Greeks were those who had been touched already by the Jewish religion, and they had a thirst for truth. Do you have a thirst for truth today? Jesus said, "Blessed are they which do hunger and thirst after righteousness: for they shall be filled" (Matthew 5:6).

God is seeking people in the world to worship his Son. Jesus said to the Samaritan woman who participated in the wrong belief, at the wrong place, with the wrong priests, "You worship what you do not know; we know what we worship, for salvation is of the Jews. But the hour is coming, and now is, when the true worshipers will worship the Father in spirit and truth; for the Father is seeking such to worship Him. God is Spirit, and those who worship Him must worship in spirit and truth" (John 4:22-24). I believe this is happening all over the world; Jesus is calling people out of false religious beliefs. Just like Jesus was calling the Samaritan woman out of her false belief to worship the true God in spirit and truth, so is He calling people today to Him.

Mary Magdalene was a believer. She arose early in the morning and went to the tomb to see Jesus. There is a certain attitude when you come to seek and worship Jesus. There must be a yearning and reaching out to Him. "Enter His gates with thanksgiving, and His courts with praise! Give thanks to Him; bless His name! For the LORD is good; his steadfast love endures forever and his faithfulness to all generations" (Psalm 100:4).

The Greeks who came to talk with Jesus had clear intent and suffered no confusion. The Bible says they presented their request to Philip at the feast. Even in worship, you can have a request for the Lord. Your worship experience affords you the privilege to ask. You can come to church and say, "Praise the Lord" and at the same time make your request of the Lord, "I need help O' Lord." Do you have a need today? Jesus is the best person to ask to help you. Just ask Him!

There is something wonderful about drawing near to Jesus. Once you get close to Him, you will never be the same. Ask the woman with the issue of blood who touched the hem of Jesus' garment and was healed. Ask the Samaritan woman with the many husbands. The man she was with was not her husband, but she experienced Jesus firsthand and became an evangelist. Ask Mary Magdalene who was delivered from seven demons. She became known as one of the greatest women of the Bible. It is important that you seek Jesus daily. The words of the prophet Jeremiah include this promise for those who seek Jesus, "Then you will call upon me and come and pray to me, and I will listen to you. You will seek me and find me when you seek me with all your heart. I will be found by you" declares the Lord, "and I will bring you back from captivity" (Jeremiah 29:12-14). Everyone needs to experience the glory of seeking the Lord. PRAISE THE LORD! AMEN.

LET'S PRAY TOGETHER

Heavenly Father,

We turn to You for all wisdom, counsel, and guidance. We are guilty of going to others before we come to seek advice from You, our Helper. We want You to be our ultimate source for all knowledge. We don't want anything to separate us from You. Help us to seek Your face and meditate on Your Word so that we can live a perfect life in and through Christ Jesus. We thank You in the name of Jesus. Amen.

Sermon Eleven

YOU CAN HAVE WHAT YOU WANT

"Believe and Trust God"
Scripture Reading: 1 Samuel 1:10-20

In bitterness of soul Hannah wept much and prayed to the LORD. And she made a vow, saying, "O LORD Almighty, if you will only look upon your servant's misery and remember me, and not forget your servant but give her a son, then I will give him to the LORD for all the days of his life, and no razor will ever be used on his head." As she kept on praying to the LORD, Eli observed her mouth. Hannah was praying in her heart, and her lips were moving but her voice was not heard. Eli thought she was drunk and said to her, "How long will you keep on getting drunk? Get rid of your wine." "Not so, my lord," Hannah replied, "I am a woman who is deeply troubled. I have not been drinking wine or beer; I was pouring out my soul to the LORD. Do not take your servant for a wicked woman;

I have been praying here out of my great anguish and grief." Eli answered, "Go in peace, and may the God of Israel grant you what you have asked of him." She said, "May your servant find favor in your eyes." Then she went her way and ate something, and her face was no longer downcast. Early the next morning they arose and worshiped before the LORD and then went back to their home at Ramah. Elkanah lay with Hannah his wife, and the LORD remembered her. So in the course of time Hannah conceived and gave birth to a son. She named him Samuel, saying, "Because I asked the LORD for him."

We hear news about the economy almost daily, and very little of what we hear is encouraging. The unemployment rate is rising, foreclosures are multiplying, debt is increasing, and financial instability is growing. Not only are we hearing about it, but many of us—including my loved ones—have been directly impacted by this. How do we respond in the face of economic challenges? For many, current economic conditions create spirits of disappointment, anxiety, and fear. But for those who are in Christ Jesus, there is a different response. Their response is to call to God Almighty, the Creator of heaven and earth. God's children place their confidence, trust, dependence, reliance, and faith in Him alone.

I want to tell you about a woman who called on God during a difficult time in her life. This woman was Hannah, the wife of Elkanah. Hannah in Hebrew means *grace* or *favor*. She was a woman who wanted to have children very much, but she was unable to conceive. Her situation is similar to other women in the Bible who were barren.

The first female who was childless in the Old Testament was Sarah, Abraham's wife. One night an angel of the Lord came to Sarah and Abraham's tent and told her that she was going to get pregnant. If you recall, Abraham and Sarah laughed because she was nearing ninety (Genesis 17:17). God kept His Word, and Sarah miraculously conceived and gave birth to a son named Isaac. Isaac's birth marked a pivotal point in the outworking of God's eternal purpose. The blessing of this son to Abraham and Sarah was part of the great step toward the fulfillment of Jehovah's plan. God's plan was to have a people of His own, separate from the surrounding nations. God wanted a people who were entrusted with His holy oracles. God wanted a people who were ultimately to become the medium of blessing to all the earth. In the realization of this plan, the first great step was the selection of Abraham to be the father of the chosen nation. This call separated him from the idolatrous people among whom he lived and caused his migration to the land which Jehovah promised to give him (Genesis 21).

The second woman who had a difficult time conceiving was Rachel, Jacob's wife. Rachel, who was Jacob's true love, was distraught that she could not give him children. She prayed and pleaded with God to bless her with a child. "Give me children or I'll die!" she demanded. After Leah, Jacob's first wife, had given birth to several sons and a daughter, God answered Rachel's prayers. She became pregnant and gave birth to a son, Joseph (Genesis 30:22). Jacob loved Joseph. Much later, she gave birth to Joseph's only full brother Benjamin, whom Jacob also loved a great deal.

The third woman is Elizabeth. In the first chapter of Luke's Gospel, we see Elizabeth and Zechariah praying to God that they might be blessed with a child. Since Elizabeth was well past childbearing age, they might have given up hope that their prayers would ever be answered. Zechariah was a priest in the temple, and one day an angel of the Lord appeared and told him that he and his wife were going to have a child, who they would name John. When Elizabeth was in her sixth month, the angel Gabriel was sent by God to her cousin Mary to announce the impending birth of Jesus. Gabriel said to Mary, "And behold, Elizabeth, your relative, has also conceived a son in her old age, and this is the sixth month for her who was called barren; for nothing will be impossible for God" (Luke 1:36). Mary immediately visited Elizabeth; Elizabeth greeted her with words which Catholics use today in their prayers to Mary, "Blessed are you among women, and blessed is the fruit of your womb" (Luke 1:42). Elizabeth was the first person to recognize Mary as the mother of the Lord, "And how does this happen to me that the mother of my Lord should come to me?" (Luke 1:43). Mary remained with Elizabeth until Elizabeth's child was born. This special child was John the Baptist, the forerunner of Jesus and one of the great prophets of the New Testament.

It is important to understand that these women's identities were tied to having children. In those days, it was considered shameful not to bear your husband's children. Women who were unable to have children were treated like an outcast and had a life without purpose and fulfillment. They did not always understand, as we do today, that it can be the husband who is infertile, rather than the wife. There were no opportunities for women to have careers or to make a name for themselves in other ways, and so most women found a sense of identity by being a wife and giving birth to many children. If they could not conceive, they felt hopeless and empty. But we know that God is able to create something from nothing. Hebrews 11:3 says, "By faith we understand that the universe was formed at God's command, so that what is seen was not made out of what was visible."

Now, we know that Hannah was one of many women that were in God's plan for redeeming His people. However, Hannah was not the only wife of Elkanah; he had another wife whose name was Penninah. This would have created an intense rivalry between these two women.

In the Old Testament, the Jewish culture practiced polygamy because warfare in ancient times was especially brutal and had an incredibly high rate of fatalities. This resulted in a greater percentage of women to men. It was nearly impossible for an unmarried woman to provide for herself as women were often uneducated and untrained. They relied on their fathers, brothers, and husbands for provision and protection. Unmarried women were often subjected to prostitution and slavery. Thus, the significant difference between the number of women and men would have left many, many women in an undesirable situation. It is possible that God may have allowed polygamy to protect and provide for the women who could not find a husband. A man would take multiple wives and serve as the provider and protector of all of them. While definitely not ideal, living in a polygamist household was far better than the alternatives: prostitution, slavery, or starvation. In addition to the protection and provision factor, polygamy enabled a much faster expansion of the nation of Israel, fulfilling God's command to "Be fruitful, and multiply, and replenish the earth, and subdue it: and have dominion over the fish of the sea, and over the fowl of the air, and over every living thing that moveth upon the earth" (Genesis 1:28). Men were capable of impregnating several women in the same time period, causing the population to grow much faster than if each man was only fathering one child each year.

However, when Jesus came to earth, He taught monogamy; there should be one woman to one man. Marriage became a godly institution. Jesus said, "But I say to you that everyone who divorces his wife, except on the ground of sexual immorality, makes her commit adultery, and whoever marries a divorced woman commits adultery" (Matthew 5:32). And He later stated, "Whoever divorces his wife, except for sexual immorality, and marries another, commits adultery" (Matthew 19:9).

Elkanah's second wife Peninnah was very fertile and conceived many children. She reminds me of Rev. John and Rena Watkins, my deceased grandparents, who raised twenty children. Can you imagine giving birth to twenty children? No doubt, Grandma Rena was fertile, too. I was told that my grandfather did two things very well: preach the gospel and produce children. My grandparents obeyed the commandments of God, "Be fruitful and increase in number; multiply on the earth."

For years, Hannah tried to conceive, but could not. She grew more and more disheartened. Peninnah added more misery to Hannah's situation by teasing and scorning her. Hannah could not eat or sleep. You see, being barren not only means being infertile, it also means feeling empty, lonely, unfruitful, isolated, unproductive and deserted. Satan uses barrenness as a crippling attempt to control one's mind. He wants you to think that God has forgotten you and has purposefully left you empty. Satan wants you to think that if you had this or that, it would make you happier. The mind is a playground for the devil, and he will put false thoughts, ideas, and suggestions in your head. Satan desires for you and me to live a lifestyle of spiritual and financial impoverishment. Jesus says, "The thief does not come except to steal, and to kill, and to destroy. I have come that they may have life, and that they may have it more abundantly" (John 10:10). Jesus came to eliminate barrenness. We don't have to feel empty anymore!

One day, Hannah went to the temple at Shiloh, and was observed by the priest Eli. Hannah was on her knees praying, petitioning, and begging God to grant her request for a child. She appealed to God, "Lord, if you give me a son, I will give him back to you as a servant." As Eli watched Hannah, he thought she was drunk. Her lips were moving, but he heard no words coming out. He said to Hannah, "Why do you come to the temple drunk, whining, complaining, crying and carrying on this way?" Hannah looked up at Eli and said, "I am not drunk. I am totally sober. I am praying to my God for help." Hannah's barrenness was too much for her to bear alone. In today's society, barrenness can represent many types of problems. It could be a financial difficulty, a life threatening illness, a crumbling marriage, losing a home, unemployment, or loved ones using an illegal substance. Whatever the barrenness is, you must do what Hannah did: pray. Hannah knew how to contact the God she served. She believed in the power of prayer. Hannah was ". . . fully persuaded that God had the power to do what he had promised" (Romans 4:21). "This is the confidence we have in approaching God: that if we ask anything according to his will, he hears us. And if we know that he hears us—whatever we ask—we know that we have what we asked of him" (1 John 5:14-15).

Hannah rose from praying with a peaceful composure. How? She put action to her faith. She believed and trusted God that He had answered her prayer. Hannah's faith did not rest in the wisdom of men (human philosophy) but in the power of God (1 Corinthians 2:5). Her faith caused her to give birth to a son. She named the boy Samuel, which means "I begged from the Lord." When Samuel became a certain age, she kept her promise to God and returned her son to Him. The same thing that God did for Hannah, He will do for you.

We are living in some tough times financially and economically, but we serve a God who "is able to do exceedingly abundantly above all that we ask or think, according to the power that works in us" (Ephesians 3:20). Psalm 84:11 says, "No good thing does the Lord withhold from those who walk uprightly." You can have what you desire if you believe and trust God! PRAISE THE LORD! AMEN.

LET'S PRAY TOGETHER

Heavenly Father,

You are all-powerful and nothing is too hard for You, not even changing the most difficult circumstances of our lives. What is impossible for us is not impossible for You, so we ask that You would do the impossible and transform us into a holy people full of Your love, peace, and joy. Enable us to do great things by the power of Your Holy Spirit. Jesus told us that if we ask You for something in His name, He will do it for us so that the Son may bring glory to the Father. All these things we ask in the name of Jesus. Amen.

Sermon Twelve

THE UNKNOWN SON

"Jesus"
Scripture Reading: Acts 17:16-23

While Paul was waiting for them in Athens, he was greatly distressed to see that the city was full of idols. So he reasoned in the synagogue with the Jews and the God-fearing Greeks, as well as in the marketplace, day by day with those who happened to be there. A group of Epicurean and Stoic philosophers began to dispute with him. Some of them asked, "What is this babbler trying to say?" Others remarked, "He seems to be advocating foreign gods." They said this because Paul was preaching the good news about Jesus and the resurrection. Then they took him and brought him to a meeting of the Areopagus, where they said to him, "May we know what this new teaching is that you are presenting? You are bringing some strange ideas to our ears, and we want to know what they mean." (All the Athenians and the foreigners who lived there

> spent their time doing nothing but talking about and listening to the latest ideas.) Paul then stood up in the meeting of the Areopagus and said: "Men of Athens! I see that in every way you are very religious. For as I walked around and looked carefully at your objects of worship, I even found an altar with this inscription: TO AN UNKNOWN GOD. Now what you worship as something unknown I am going to proclaim to you."

In our scripture reading, the Apostle Paul is in the city of Athens, Greece. Paul's visit to Athens was part of what is generally referred to as his second missionary journey. This journey began after the Jerusalem Council was held, at which time the Jerusalem elders and the apostles concluded that the Gentile converts did not have to convert to Judaism in order to become Christians. Christianity was distinguished from Judaism even though salvation came through Judaism. The early Christians paved the way for even more extensive evangelism among the Gentiles.

The city of Athens was filled with scholars, philosophers, and poets—intellectual types who followed the teachings of Plato, Aristotle, and Socrates. Athens was also filled with many idols, statues and altars dedicated to every god and goddess that you could imagine. Some of the Greek gods and goddesses were Athena, goddess of wisdom and civilization; Poseidon, god of the sea; Artemis, goddess of nature; Ares, god of war; Aphrodite, goddess of love; and lastly Zeus, the chief god of order. Greeks worshipped them because they believed that the blessings of protection, food, shelter and prosperity came from their provisions. It reminds me of the many gods that people worship today. Our economy is in terrible shape, and part of the reason is because we worship creation instead of the Creator. Created things were never meant to be substituted for the Creator. God did not create this world to be excommunicated from it. God said, "You shall have no other gods before me" (Exodus 20:3).

Paul noticed that the people of Athens were very religious because of their many idols and statues. He told the people of Athens, "I noticed you believe in worship because there are many altars, even one dedicated to 'AN UNKNOWN GOD.'" The text says that Paul was provoked in his spirit. He was angry and highly upset because everywhere he looked he saw idolatry, and the core of idolatry is putting something else in the place of Christ. Paul could not stand Christ not being glorified. Paul's burden was not that lost people were dying, although I am sure that he knew that and it pained him. He was not provoked by the temple prostitution, Athens' corrupt politics, divorce, or the infanticide of children. It was that the city had given itself over to idols instead of Christ that pushed him over the edge. He knew that Jesus deserves all the glory because He gave us both life and redemption: "I am the Lord; that is my name! I will not give my glory to another or my praise to idols" (Isaiah 42:8).

Idolatry is not a practice isolated to ancient cultures; it is also prevalent in our culture. We see its manifestation through addictions, and its fatal effects every day. People seek the thrill of drugs to attain happiness, only to drop into the shaky depression of addiction. They view alcohol as the answer to wash away their cares and give them courage, calmness, or prestige, but it inevitably leaves them painfully hung over and abused. Careers and occupations are admirable goals, but they too can become elevated to the point where one eats, drinks, and breathes work. Student grades can also become everything. Some students sacrifice everything for the sake of studying, leaving the rest of their lives in shambles. Likewise, relationships are a common substitute for God. We put friends, mentors, partners, spouses, or even children on pedestals that they were never meant to be on. We even put our pets and material things on pedestals. Sadly, many people omit the whole person and desire an act or service, such as prostitution, pornography, adultery, and fornication. In all of these cases, something or someone is sought after, desired, and idolized. In every case mentioned, an object is pursued in the hopes of filling a void or finding lasting joy. How sad it is that people think these things can bring them joy. Remember what Jesus said, "The thief comes only to steal and kill and destroy; I have come that they may have life, and have it to the full" (John 10:10). If you think that people or things can fill your emptiness and give you peace and joy, you are spiritually blind. Only in the Lord Jesus Christ can life be truly fulfilling and satisfying. King David says just as the deer pants for streams of water, our soul should pant for the Lord. And our soul should thirst for God and desire to spend time with Him (Psalm 42:1-2). The Prophet Isaiah informs us to delight greatly in the Lord and rejoice in God (Isaiah 61:10).

Living From Faith To Faith

No matter where Paul visited, he seldom passed up an invitation to preach the gospel to lost men and women. The opportunity to speak in the synagogue was apparently a matter of custom, but an invitation to preach to pagan philosophers was rare. This uncommon offer was given to Paul in Athens. As Paul spoke in the marketplace, he drew the attention of both the Epicurean and Stoic. He began to share his powerful testimony about his experiences with the Lord—their so-called "unknown God." Paul said that one day he heard the voice of the Lord speaking to Him. "Saul! Saul! (his original name) Why do you persecute me?" "Who are you, Lord?" I asked. "I am Jesus of Nazareth, whom you are persecuting," he replied. My companions saw the light, but they did not understand the voice of Him who was speaking to me. "What shall I do, Lord?" I asked. "Get up," the Lord said, "and go into Damascus. There you will be told all that you have been assigned to do" (Acts 9:4-6). I can only imagine what was going through Paul's mind as he tried to explain to his listeners about Christ. Paul told them to pay attention; the Lord God was not in some far-off place a billion miles away. No, this God was named Jesus, and He was near. He was so near that He lived in the hearts of every believer. Paul preached long and hard to the listeners. "The world cannot accept Him, because it neither sees Him nor knows Him. But you know Him, for He lives with you and will be in you" (John 14:17). "But he who unites Himself with the Lord is one with Him in spirit" (1 Corinthians 6:17). This God demands and desires the praises of His people. "Enter his gates with thanksgiving and His courts with praise, give thanks to Him and praise His name" (Psalm 100:4). I am sure Paul continued to explain in his testimony that "God is Spirit, and His worshipers must worship in spirit and truth" (John 4:24). In John 3:5-6, Jesus said, "I tell you the truth, no one can enter the kingdom of God unless he is born of water and the Spirit. Flesh gives birth to flesh, but the Spirit gives birth to spirit."

Paul was getting deep into witnessing about Jesus when he decided to share the creation story that God created the heavens and the earth, and all that is in them. He made man out of the dust of the earth, and breathed life into man. God made both man and woman; He instructed them to dominate and populate the earth. Paul told them that God enjoys fellowship with His people; however, when man sinned, he lost that perfect fellowship. But thanks be to God, He had a plan to restore humanity back to Him by sending His Son Jesus to redeem the world! Paul began to explain to his listeners about the birth of Jesus. He informed them that Jesus was born of a virgin named Mary. He was conceived by the Holy Ghost. He was not born of man, but of God. John 3:16, says, "For God so loved the world that he gave his only begotten Son, that whoever believes in him shall not perish, but have eternal life." Like the Athenians, you need to understand that this Jesus was God in the flesh!

At the age of thirty, Jesus was baptized in the Jordan River by John the Baptist. The Holy Ghost descended in a bodily shape like a dove upon Him, and a voice came from heaven: "You are my Son, whom I love; with you I am well pleased" (Luke 3:22). This was a perfect picture of the trinity of God united as one: God the Father, God the Son, and God the Holy Spirit. After the baptism, Jesus was led into the wilderness by the

Spirit of God, where He was tempted by Satan. Jesus defeated Satan with the Word of God. Jesus answered, "It is written: 'Worship the Lord your God and serve Him only'" (Luke 4:8). He then visited the synagogue in the city of Nazareth, and read the scroll from the Prophet Isaiah 61:1-2: "The Spirit of the Sovereign LORD is on me, because the LORD has anointed me to preach good news to the poor. He has sent me to bind up the brokenhearted, to proclaim freedom for the captives, and to release from darkness for the prisoners, to proclaim the year of the LORD's favor and the day of vengeance of our God, to comfort all who mourn." Jesus closed the book and told the crowd, "Today, this scripture has been fulfilled in your ears." Jesus came down through forty-two generations to do what man could not do. He wanted to restore the fellowship and relationship that man once had with God.

Jesus went from city to city preaching the kingdom of God and healing the sick as did Paul. Jesus healed a man who had leprosy and cast out demons, making people whole. Jesus gave sight to a man born blind and raised Jarius' daughter from the dead. From the grave, He also raised Lazarus, a man who was dead for four days. He told Lazarus's sister Martha, "I am the resurrection, and the life: he that believeth in me, though he were dead, yet shall he live: And whosoever liveth and believeth in me shall never die" (John 11:25-26). Jesus looked at them and said, "With man this is impossible, but with God all things are possible" (Mark 10:27).

Jesus commissioned His disciples to teach all nations about the kingdom of God, baptizing the people in the name of the Father, the Son, and the Holy Ghost. He made a promise to

His disciples that holds for us today: "And surely I am with you always, to the very end of the age" (Matthew 28:20). Jesus had a destiny. His destiny carried Him to His cross at Calvary where He died for the sins of the world. Isaiah 53:5-7 quotes, "But he was pierced for our transgressions, he was crushed for our iniquities; the punishment that brought us peace was upon him, and by his wounds we are healed. We all, like sheep, have gone astray, each of us has turned to his own way; and the LORD has laid on him the iniquity of us all. He was oppressed and afflicted, yet he did not open his mouth; he was led like a lamb to the slaughter, and as a sheep before her shearers is silent, so he did not open his mouth." His body was put into the tomb and sealed with a stone, but after three days, Jesus arose from the grave to conquer death and hell.

At the beginning of the next week, Mary Magdalene and the other women got up early one morning to visit the tomb of Jesus. There was a great earthquake, and an angel of the Lord rolled back the stone from the tomb. The angel told the women not to fear, and that Jesus was not there because He had risen. As they were running to tell the other disciples, Jesus met them and said, "Do not be afraid. Go and tell my brothers to go to Galilee; there they will see me." (Matthew 28:10). Jesus met with all who believed in Him and filled them with the Holy Spirit, as prophesied by Joel: "And afterward, I will pour out my Spirit on all people. Your sons and daughters will prophesy, your old men will dream dreams, your young men will see visions. Even on my servants, both men and women, I will pour out my Spirit in those days" (Joel 2:28-29). When the Lord Himself came to earth as God the Son, His intent was to create a new nation in which everyone would receive the Holy Spirit and become one family in the body of Christ.

The message Paul preached in Athens is the same one we preach today: Jesus' resurrection. Without the resurrection, there is no gospel, no salvation, and no eternal life. Thank God we can say with great confidence that God raised His Son, Jesus, from the grave and He lives forever. After Paul preached the gospel of Jesus Christ, I'm sure that he told them to stop worshipping idols and take down the sign that read "AN UNKNOWN GOD," for now they knew the God who deserved their worship.

I want you to know today, "that you are a chosen people, a royal priesthood, a holy nation, a people belonging to God, that you may declare the praises of Him who called you out of darkness into his wonderful light" (1 Peter 2:9). Our Lord does have a name, and His name is Jesus! PRAISE THE LORD! AMEN.

LET'S PRAY TOGETHER

Heavenly Father,

You are the God of the universe and the Lord of our lives. We worship You and give glory to Jesus. Jesus' resurrection gave us the power to experience true joy, peace, prosperity, and daily fellowship with You. We cherish each day because we are in Jesus and He is in us. Because Your Word said that You are able to do beyond what we can even imagine and

Dr. Gloria Ann Turner

ask, we call on You to meet all our needs in ways more wonderful than we can even hope. We ask these things in Jesus' name. Amen.

CONCLUSION

In the introduction, I prayed these sermons would strengthen your faith and deepen your commitment to serve the Lord. For greater understanding and a spiritual transformation, it is important for you to return to these pages to study parts of the sermons carefully. I am confident that you will continue to experience not only an increase in faith, but also the presence of God in a greater dimension.

In these sermons, I have shared many powerful doctrines regarding God's sovereign will for you. God desires for you to partner with Him in the greater purpose of reclaiming and redeeming the world. The Scripture says, "If my people, who are called by my name, will humble themselves and pray and seek my face and turn from their wicked ways, then will I hear from heaven and will forgive their sin and will heal their land" (2 Chronicles 7:14). God is saying, "*If* my people . . . *then* will I." You must make the first move by faith toward God and only then will He reveal and execute His promise, purpose, and power in your life.

Truly, the Bible is our source of inspiration, guidance, and right living. The answers we seek are within those sacred pages. The more time we spend studying the Word, the more God will reveal Himself to us through His Son Jesus.

God loves you, God blesses you, and God appreciates you, and so do I!

ABOUT THE AUTHOR

Dr. Gloria Ann Turner is a multi-gifted motivational speaker, author, professor, and leadership mentor. She is the founder and president of *Faith to Faith Ministries* (www.ftfministries.com), a prophetic ministry that teaches the supernatural power of God. She was ordained in the African Methodist Episcopal Church as an Elder in 2001.

Dr. Turner earned a Master of Arts Degree in Religious Studies from Howard University, Washington, D.C.; a Master of Divinity from Wesley Theological Seminary, Washington, D. C.; and a Doctorate of Theology at Chesapeake Bible College and Seminary of Ridgely, Maryland. Her theological studies focused on two primary concerns: Faith in the African American Family and The Manifestation of the Spiritual Gifts of the Holy Spirit. Her concentration focuses not only on proclaiming the gospel message, but on spiritual development, Christian education, and community outreach.

A believer in the empowerment of education, she is also the founder and president of *The Watkins Foundation*, an educational and a community outreach program that counsels students to become future achievers.

Dr. Gloria Ann Turner

When she is not traveling or speaking, Dr. Turner's treasured moments are spent with her family. She lives in Maryland with her husband Robert, daughter TiNese, son Michael, daughter-in-law Nailah, and grandson Brandon.

Her favorite scripture is Matthew 19:26, "With men it is impossible, but with God all things are possible."